Massacre on the River Raisin

Massacre on the River Raisin

Three Accounts of the Disastrous Michigan Campaign During the War of 1812

Narrative of the Suffering & Defeat of the North-Western Army Under General Winchester
William Atherton

A Journal
Elias Darnell

Harrison and Procter: The River Raisin
E. A. Cruikshank

LEONAUR

Massacre on the River Raisin
Three Accounts of the Disastrous Michigan Campaign During the War of 1812
Narrative of the Suffering & Defeat of the North-Western Army Under General
Winchester
by William Atherton
A Journal
by Elias Darnell
and
Harrison and Procter: The River Raisin
by E. A. Cruikshank

FIRST EDITION

First published under the titles
Narrative of the Suffering & Defeat of the North-Western Army Under General
Winchester
A Journal Containing an Accurate and Interesting Account of the Hardships,
Sufferings, Battles, Defeat, and Captivity of Those Heroic Kentucky Volunteers and
Regulars, Commanded by General Winchester, in the Years 1812-1813. Also, Two
Narratives, by Men That Were Wounded in the Battles on the River Raisin, and Taken
Captive by the Indians.
and
Harrison and Proctor: The River Raisin

Leonaur is an imprint
of Oakpast Ltd

ISBN: 978-1-78282-132-8 (hardcover)
ISBN: 978-1-78282-133-5 (softcover)

http://www.leonaur.com

Publisher's Notes
The views expressed in this book are not necessarily
those of the publisher.

Contents

Narrative of the Suffering & Defeat of the North-Western
Army Under General Winchester   7

A Journal   83

Harrison and Procter: The River Raisin   145

Narrative of the Suffering & Defeat of the North-Western Army Under General Winchester

Contents

Preface   11

Narrative   13

Kentucky Mothers   80

Preface

The greater part of this short narrative was written years ago. At that time it was intended for publication. But for several years past the writer had declined ever letting it come before the world; and had it not been for the solicitations of friends, it is highly probable this intention would never have been changed. But relying upon the opinion of those whom he believed to be well qualified to judge of it, and believing them to be sincere in their expression of opinion, I have consented to let it go and take its chance before the public.

It was found difficult to give such an account of that part of the campaign which it was thought to be most important, without commencing as far back as the departure of the army from Kentucky. This part of the history has, however, been passed over very rapidly, perhaps rather too much so to make it at all satisfactory. The writer is aware that he has omitted much which would have added to the interest of this little history; but he has not leisure to go over it again. History has given us an account of the sufferings of the North-Western Army only in general terms, but nowhere, so far as I have been able to learn, has there been given a particular detail of the sufferings and privations of that detachment of the army.

I think it proper that the rising generation should know what their fathers suffered, and how they acted in the hour of danger; that they sustained the double character of "*Americans and Kentuckians.*" This narrative has been made as concise as I could conveniently make it, and on that account, perhaps, the writer has not said all that might, and that should have been said. But it is hoped that what has been said will be sufficient to give the youthful reader some idea of what that "Spartan band" were called to endure. To the old men of our country these things, perhaps, will not be new.

With regard to the massacre at Raisin, the writer has related nothing but what he saw. What is said in reference to the brave Hart and Hickman, he witnessed with his own eyes.

It may be thought that I have been a little too severe in what I have said of British officers. Should any think so, all I have to say is, had they seen and felt what we did there would have been no difference of opinion. By some it will be thought strange to find the savages, in point of feeling and humanity, placed above the British—but the truth ought always to be told.

One thing the writer regrets, and that is his being compelled so frequently to speak of himself. But he found it impossible to give a full narration without it. Nothing is aimed at but a plain unvarnished statement of facts, a sober description of scenes, in the principal part of which the writer himself was an actor.

Narrative

The volunteers from Kentucky, under the command of Colonels Allen, Lewis and Scott, left their homes on the 12th of August, 1812, and rendezvoused at Georgetown. Thence took the Dry Ridge road to Cincinnati, where we remained a few days. We then pursued our march through the State of Ohio, by the way of Piqua; from which place we were called to the relief of Fort Wayne.

Nothing worthy of public notice occurred on the way, except the alarm we had at the camp we called "Fighton," which every soldier that was on the ground no doubt recollects. Though we were alarmed at Piqua, by one of the sentinels shooting at a horse, yet we had seen nothing such as occurred here. It was a dark rainy night, just such a time as the Indians would choose to make an attack. We anticipated danger, and made arrangements to meet it. The army encamped in a hollow square, within a strong breastwork, and guards were placed at every point. Whether there were Indians about or not, some of the guard thought they heard them, and many guns were fired on post, and all the camp called to arms. The line of battle was more than once formed during the night, and at one time kept under arms an hour and a half.

As this was the first campaign with most of us, and also the first alarm worthy of notice, it is not easy to imagine the degree of excitement produced throughout the camp. It fell to my lot to be on guard that night, and at the time of the greatest alarm was on post; the guard was not relieved for near an hour after their time had expired—an attack being momently expected.

When we arrived at Fort Wayne, we found that the Indians which had annoyed the fort for some time, had retreated. We were then ordered to march to two Indian towns, for the purpose of burning the houses and destroying their corn. When we had accomplished this, and returned to Fort Wayne, we there met the Kentucky mounted volunteers under the command of Colonel Simrall. We marched from Fort Wayne on the 22nd of September, and pursued Wayne's route down the Miami towards old Fort Defiance, where we arrived on the 30th. During the latter part of this march we were frequently annoyed by the enemy. Our advance party of spies fell in with a body of Indians, and a small skirmish ensued, in which one of the spies was slightly wounded, and several of the enemy killed; the exact number could not be ascertained, as the Indians always carry off their dead when practicable.

The day before, Ensign Liggett, of the regulars, with four men, was pursued by this body of Indians, massacred and scalped. The loss of Ensign Liggett was much lamented, as he was a promising young officer, remarkable for bravery and intrepidity. He had left the company of spies, with his four companions, to examine the country around Fort Defiance, and had advanced several miles ahead of the party—where they were killed. Many of Ensign Liggett's friends are still living in Kentucky, (as at time of first publication).

The annoyance from the enemy greatly retarded our movements, as it was impossible, with any degree of certainty, to ascertain either their situation or force. In crossing the river, however, their whole movements were discovered. The British, with their artillery from Detroit, and a large party of Indians, were progressing towards Fort Wayne. After engaging our spies, and annoying our advanced guard, they faced to the right about and retreated precipitately. Owing to the situation of the army (being short of provisions) it was impossible, by forced marches, to intercept them. At this time Captain Bland Ballard showed his skill in Indian fighting, by making good his retreat, for which he deserves much. His lieutenant, Munday, who had parted with him in the morning, also effected a retreat, by charging upon the Indians, before they ascertained his numbers, and then dashing into camp.

The next day our spies had an action—had one wounded—and saw several Indians fall. The day following the Indians showed in front of the spies, and snapped at one of our men—a fire was returned, which left blood where the Indians stood. The Indian spies were on horseback, which rendered it difficult to ascertain their situation. Our spies could not, with propriety, venture far from us, and we could not advance until the country was reconnoitred, consequently our march was slow. A short turn to the right, however, and crossing the river at an unexpected place, gave us the advantage. After crossing the river we saw that the enemy had artillery, and were ahead of us. We were now within six miles of Defiance. It was very bushy for more than a mile before we approached the fort.

The army remained at camp that morning, and sent out spies in every direction; when they returned, they reported that the enemy had gone off down the river. It was then deemed inexpedient to move so late in the afternoon. It was supposed there were from one to two hundred British, with from two to five pieces of cannon, and from four to six hundred Indians. The artillery was certainly brought up by water to this place, and re-embarked here again. Their object must have been Fort Wayne. By this time we became very scarce of provisions, having nothing for some days but the poorest beef. Some of the men began to murmur—and some went so far as to talk of returning home—but when this was known by the officers, measures were taken to put a stop to it. Colonel Allen, in an animated and encouraging address to his men, banished the idea of shrinking in the day of adversity. Captain Simpson, also, was not unemployed. This was the first time we had sensibly felt the want of bread.

General Harrison returned to the army on the second of October. We were greatly animated at seeing him among us once more. He addressed the whole army in a most thrilling speech, which kindled in the breasts of the men, generally, an increased desire to meet the enemy, and a willingness to endure any privations they might be called to suffer. He remained with us but a short time.

The enemy having retreated before us in every direction, leaving us an extensive territory to occupy; our object then was to establish a chain of fortified posts, in order to facilitate the supplies necessary for a speedy invasion of Upper Canada. Notwithstanding we were in the enemy's country, where Indian spies were seen almost every day, yet it was impossible to keep the men from imprudently hazarding their lives! Shortly after our arrival at Fort Defiance, five of our men, who had been out gathering plums, were found scalped. About this time Captain Garrard's troop of horse, and another company, met a scouting party of Indians and routed them.

One of our militia was killed and another wounded. In consequence of this information, General Harrison marched the whole of his army from St. Mary's to Defiance. General Harrison had heard from General Kelso, who commanded a detachment of troops on lake Erie, that *two thousand* Indians and some regulars with several pieces of artillery, had left Malden on an expedition against Fort Wayne! This news, with other exaggerated accounts, induced the belief that General Winchester was likely to be defeated. As before stated, all the forces at St. Mary's were put in motion, but before they reached Defiance information of the enemy's retreat was received.

Before General Harrison left Defiance, he selected a situation for a new fort. A party of men was detailed to procure timber for the buildings. General Winchester, also, moved his camp from the Miami to the Auglaize River.

The command of the left was now confided to General Winchester, who was instructed to occupy the rapids as soon as possible for the purpose of securing a quantity of corn which had been raised by the inhabitants.

Before General Harrison left, he ordered General Tupper to take all his mounted men and proceed down the Miami as far as the Rapids. When this order was issued, General Tupper's command was immediately supplied with provision for eight days, which included all the flour in camp. About 12 o'clock next day a party of Indians fired on the men immediately on the opposite bank of the Miami, one of whom they killed, scalped, and then fled! This, for a moment, produced alarm, and the troops were formed in order of battle. Presently small parties of horsemen began to cross the river in pursuit of the enemy. The horses were mostly at grass, and as soon as they could be caught the owners engaged in the pursuit.

Eight or ten parties went, mostly from Colonel Simrall's regiment, in one of which was the colonel himself. General Tupper ordered that no more should cross, apprehending from the boldness of the Indians that a large body might be lying in ambush. General Winchester now ordered Tupper to commence his expedition towards the Rapids by pursuing these Indians. Tupper had previously sent Logan and six other Indians to reconnoitre, and did not seem willing to go until they returned. They arrived in the evening, stating that they had seen a party of Indians, about fifty strong, ten miles down the river. Colonel Allen now offered his services to accompany Tupper to the Rapids in any station he thought proper to place him, from a private soldier upwards. He accepted his offer, and caused him to be announced as his aid. General Winchester issued positive orders that General Tupper should proceed; but he declined, saying he would prefer going by the Ottoway towns, &c.

At this time about three hundred of the mounted riflemen, whose

16

terms of service had expired, left the camp and returned home. Colonel Simrall, believing that the orders of General Winchester to General Tupper would not be executed, returned to the settlements to recruit his horses and be in readiness to march when his services should be necessary. It will be sufficient to say this expedition at this time failed. After the mounted men left us, nothing of importance occurred for some time. We were engaged building the fort, which, through much difficulty, was at length completed. This will appear, when it is known that at that place we had not our full rations. That this fact may be established, I will give some extracts from a letter, written at the time, by James Garrard, Brigade Inspector:

> We have no drawn a full ration since the 8th September. Sometimes without beef—at other times without flour: and the worst of all, entirely without salt, which has been much against the health of the men. They bear it with much patience, although they have been without salt for five or six days.

At this time the sick amounted to two hundred and sixteen men, and there was some dissatisfaction in the army against the government because the necessary supplies were not sent on. But when they became acquainted with the true cause of the deficiency, that the fault was not in the government, but in the change of affairs since their march, they were perfectly satisfied. Again Mr. Garrard states:

> You would be surprised to see the men appear on the brigade parade. Some without shoes, others without socks, blankets, &c. All the clothes they have are linen; but they discharge their duty with cheerfulness, hoping that their country will supply their wants before the severity of winter comes on.

There are many who can testify to the truth of the above. What clothes we took with us when we left our homes had worn very thin. Many left home with their linen hunting shirts, and some of these were literally torn to rags by the brush. We had heard that General Harrison had made a powerful appeal to the ladies of Kentucky and Ohio, and we were sure it would not be in vain; and about this time we learned that the ladies of Kentucky were exerting themselves to relieve the soldiers of this army. It was highly gratifying to us to know that we were kept in remembrance by the ladies of our own State.

Near this time our spies brought in a prisoner. They took him about thirty miles below Fort Winchester. He called himself William

Walker; had been with the Indians near thirty years, and was married to a Wyandott squaw; he said at that time he lived at Detroit. He was recognized by several in camp, and two men said, "when Detroit was taken, under General Hull, he was painted like an Indian, and was seen out of the fort," but they did not recollect any act of hostility on his part. His story was, that he persuaded the Indians to abandon the British; that in the end we would ruin them, &c. That for this he was put into the guard-house at Detroit, and told his conduct was criminal, and consequently would be sent where he would be kept safely; that he made his escape from the guard-house—lay concealed a few days until he was ready—and then started to join us.

The general belief was he came as a spy. He seemed intimately acquainted with the Indian movements, but the officers were afraid to place any reliance upon his statements. He gave us a description of the force we met near Defiance on their way to Fort Wayne. He estimated their number at about nine hundred Indians and British altogether, with two brass field pieces; that the afternoon on which we crossed the Miami, they were at Fort Defiance, which was only six miles from where we crossed the river, and that they started early next morning towards the rapids. From him we learned that McCoy of Georgetown, whom we supposed was murdered, had been taken prisoner. Upon being asked if any prisoners had been taken, he replied one—a quarter master sergeant. McCoy filled that place.

We now began preparations to march towards the Rapids—having completed a new and beautiful fort, situated near the old one, which, like its brave progenitor, had fallen before the irresistible hand of time. We crossed the Miami, and camped a few miles below Defiance. During the time of our encampment we were called to witness a very solemn transaction. A young man was found sleeping on post—he was arraigned and sentenced to be shot. When the time appointed for his execution arrived, the army was paraded—the prisoner was brought to the spot—a bandage placed over his eyes—and directed to prepare to meet death. A platoon was ordered to take their stand a few paces in front of the lines, ready to fire when the word should be given.

A deep silence now reigned throughout the army—every eye was fixed upon the criminal, standing upon his knees blindfolded—the officer commanding the platoon waiting to hear and give the word which would hurry a fellow soldier into eternity. During this moment of suspense a messenger came from the general bearing a reprieve. This circumstance made a deep impression upon the whole army. It was found necessary, also, to make an example of one who had deserted. His sentence was to ride the wooden horse; which was made by bending a sapling until the top reached the ground—this he did in the presence of the whole army.

Very few Indians were seen or heard of for some weeks, neither had any mischief been done, though the men were very careless, and would hunt game and fruit far and near—often strolling miles from the camp without guns. The ground on this side of the river, where we first encamped, being disagreeable, we marched a few miles down the river, remained a short time, and then removed to what is called camp No. 3. There we had a beautiful situation, and an abundance of fine timber.

Although the enemy had now retreated and left us in possession of the Territory, we were still called to contend with the severe weather, which not only prevented the necessary supply of provisions from reaching us, but in our thinly clad condition became very oppressive. We knew that efforts were making to supply us with clothes and rations, but the roads were almost impassable. About the first of November the men became very sickly—the typhus fever raged with violence—three or four would sometimes die in a day. It is said upwards of three hundred was on the sick list at one time.

Towards the latter part of November, or first of December, the rain fell in torrents. We were ordered to build huts, for to advance at that time appeared impossible. Many were so entirely destitute of shoes and other clothing, that had they been compelled to march any distance they must have frozen. What we suffered at Defiance was but the beginning of affliction. We now saw nothing but hunger, and cold, and nakedness, staring us in the face. At one time, for several days, we scarcely had anything to eat but some poor beef. I have seen the butchers go to a beef and kill it, when lying down and could not get out of the way. This kind of beef, and hickory roots, was our principal subsistence for a length of time. When we had been here a few weeks, and the ground became covered with snow, and we no longer apprehended danger from the enemy, we were permitted to hunt. This we did to some extent, but in a short time there was not a squirrel to be found near the encampment.

During our stay at camp No. 3, a detachment was sent down the river to assist General Tupper. I was one of the number called out for that expedition; and a hard and fruitless one it was. Colonel Lewis commanded. We marched until about nine o'clock at night. Colonel

C. S. Todd, with some others, was sent on to Tupper's encampment to make some discoveries, and when they arrived at the spot they found that Tupper had retreated, and one of his men left dead in the camp! This information was brought to Colonel Lewis, and after a council with his officers, he considered it prudent to return. He thought if it were necessary for Tupper, with six hundred and fifty men, to retreat, and the river too between him and the enemy, he could not be justified in meeting it on the same side with three hundred and eighty. It was stated, but I would not vouch for the truth of it, that he left the rapids a few hours after he sent the express to our camp, without notifying our detachment at all.

Early next morning we commenced our retreat, but from the fatigues of the previous day, and want of rest that night, (for we had no fire,) the most of us were unable to reach the army that day, but were obliged to camp about five miles below. This was a night of keen suspense to myself, and no doubt many others. We had grounds to believe the Indians would pursue us with perhaps double our number, and surprise us in the night; but we reached the camp in safety next morning.

Our Indian spies made frequent excursions in different directions, but their reports were not generally satisfactory. Logan, one of the finest looking Indians I ever saw, was one of them, and perhaps the only honest man among them, finding that they were suspected either of cowardice or treachery, determined on another expedition to the rapids. But before leaving, expressed his grief at the stain cast upon his character—declaring at the same time that something should be done before his return that should convince all concerned of his bravery and friendship to the Government of the United States. Old Captain John, and Lightfoot, if I mistake not, accompanied him. They had not reached the rapids before they fell in with the spies of the British—a company of Indians superior to their own, commanded by a young British officer: they managed the affair with great dexterity.

Logan, who was a man of great presence of mind, finding, upon first sight of the enemy, a retreat to be impracticable, instantly proposed to his comrades to approach them in the character of friends, and report themselves as deserters from camp No. 3. Though they had but a very few moments, yet Logan fixed upon the signal, and concerted the plan of escape. They met—Logan made his statement, which was received cautiously, but so far as to prevent immediate hostilities. They were permitted to keep their arms, but ordered to march in front, a plain indication that they were suspected.

As the object of this band of British spies was to gain information in reference to the army at camp No. 3, they considered their object accomplished, and therefore returned from this place. A conversation soon commenced respecting the condition, number, and intentions of the army, &c., &c., during which time Logan and his two companions were watching their opportunity to make the attack. Although they doubled their number, yet they determined to *rescue themselves or die.* The signal was given, and each man brought his man to the ground. This left their power about equal. The enemy fled a little distance, and opened a fire upon them, which they returned with the arms of those they had shot; but finding a retreat now practicable, Logan ordered it, but in mounting one of the horses of the enemy, received a ball in his breast which ranged down to the small of his back; but, notwithstanding, succeeded in reaching the camp that night, a distance of about thirty miles.

Old Captain John would not leave the spot until he had taken a scalp, which he brought to camp with him. Every effort was made by the physicians to save the life of this brave and daring man, but all in vain. I saw him a few hours before his death. He died like a soldier. But before his death, was heard to say—"I suppose this will be taken as evidence of my bravery, and I shall be no longer suspected as a traitor."

His death was greatly lamented, and his loss severely felt—and the circumstances taken altogether, rendered the case exceedingly affecting, especially to some of the officers.

One of the most extraordinary characters in all the army, was an old man by the name of Ruddle who acted as a spy; this man made many excursions alone, and would remain for several days together, almost in the heart of the enemy; and perhaps advanced farther to discover the movements of the British and Indians, than even our Indian spies. During the stay at camp No. 3, the most of the information that could be relied upon, respecting the supplies which it was expected we should find in the fields at the rapids, came through Ruddle. Such dauntless courage is not often found. To look at him you would think him touched off a little with the Potawatamie. He was well acquainted with the Indian mode of warfare; and, if I mistake not, had once been a prisoner among them.

Soon after this the river was frozen so as to bear us across. This enlarged our hunting ground, for now we were suffering greatly for provisions. At one time, for eleven days, we had nothing but pork, just killed, without salt. These privations were submitted to with astonishing patience—there was scarcely a whisper or a murmur in all the camp—which manifested a patriotism worthy the cause in which they were engaged. On the 22nd of December we were informed, by general order, that we should have flour that day, and that the prospect was fair for a constant supply.

The 24th was the period set for our stay at camp No. 3, which was pleasing intelligence to the whole army. On the 25th, at sunrise, we were commanded to march to the rapids. Being the vanguard of the North-Western Army, General Harrison instructed us to make a stand there until we should be joined by the North-Western Army. For some time previous we had been engaged in making sleds to haul our baggage, some of which had to be drawn by the soldiers themselves.

A more pleasant and expeditious march than this had been anticipated, for after much fatigue and labour, a great number of canoes had been made, with which we expected our baggage would be taken with great ease and safety down the river; but to our great disappointment, before we could make preparations, or before our provisions reached us—without which we could not move—cold weather set in, and closed up the river. This circumstance at first seemed to present an obstacle insurmountable; many of the men were sick, and that sickness occasioned by being compelled to eat fresh pork without bread or salt, and from being exposed to cold and wet.

But this was not the only difficulty. Many who had not been so provident, perhaps, as the case required, were bare of clothes, and almost barefooted, and were ill prepared to undertake such a march through the snow.

Thus, ill clad, worn down by fatigue and starvation, and chilled by the cold wintry blasts of the north we were compelled to brave—there was no alternative—our condition made it necessary for us to fall upon some other plan to reach the rapids, where we expected to meet supplies. Under the impulse of this hope we went to work and made sleds sufficient to carry the baggage. But as these were not sufficient to take the sick, many of them had to be left behind. On the 25th, as above stated, we bid *adieu* to this memorable place, camp No. 3, where lie the bones of many a brave man. This place will live in the recollection of all who suffered there, and for more reasons than one.

There comes up before the mind the many times the dead march was heard in the camp, and the solemn procession that carried our fellow sufferers to the grave—the many times we were almost on the point of starvation—and the many sickening disappointments which were experienced by the army from day to day, and from week to week, by the failure of promised supplies, which were daily expected: and, also, that here we parted with the sick, some of whom we were to see no more.

Thus poorly equipped, deeply affected, and yet overjoyed, we took up the line of march. The reader may ask how such a number of sleds could be drawn, seeing there was not a supply of horses. Some of them were drawn by the *men themselves*—five men were hitched to a sleigh, and, through snow and water, dragged them on at the rate of about ten miles a day. But to our great disadvantage during our march, there was an immense fall of snow. It seemed that the very elements fought against us. But notwithstanding all, we moved slowly on towards the destined point. What the men suffered by day, was comparatively nothing to what they experienced by night. The reader can form but a faint idea unless he had been on the spot, and had seen and felt what we saw and felt.

Some time was required to arrange the encampment, during which time the men were compelled to keep their places in the lines, and thus become so chilled as to be almost unfit for the necessary exertion of preparing a resting place for themselves. The snow, which was about knee deep, had first to be cleared away, then fire to be struck with flint and steel, and when no lynn bark could be had, brush was substituted in its place, which formed our bed. Hard and uncomfortable as it was, yet such was our fatigue that we generally slept soundly. To give a detailed account of individual suffering during this march, from camp No. 3 to the rapids, would swell this sketch beyond its intended limits; and perhaps facts would be related which the present generation, who have but little knowledge of these things only from report, would scarcely believe.

Our little vehicles being made upon a small scale, were too light to carry the burden put upon them, and not sufficiently high to cross the little streams which lay in our way, consequently much damage was done to our baggage, and our provisions (which were barely sufficient to last us to the rapids,) was much injured by getting wet. This, it will be plainly seen, was well calculated to increase our sufferings. In fact, the half of what was endured on this slow and painful march has never yet been published to the world, and perhaps never will.

While on our march, General Winchester received another despatch from the commander-in-chief, recommending him to abandon the movement towards the Rapids, and fall back with the greater part of his force to Fort Jennings. This advice was given in consequence of some intelligence received from Colonel Campbell, at Massiniway, respecting the force of Tecumseh on the Wabash. General Harrison was apprehensive if the left wing advanced so far as the rapids, Tecumseh would be able to attack and destroy all the provisions in the rear.

Winchester had already commenced his march, and did not wish to discontinue and return.

At length, on the 10th of January, we arrived at the rapids. General Winchester had previously sent forward a detachment of six hundred and seventy men, under General Payne, to attack a body of Indians which General Harrison had been informed was lying in an old fortification at Swan creek, a few miles farther down the river. After passing several miles below the old fort, and discovering no appearance of Indians, the whole returned to the position which the army intended to occupy.

About this time the clothes which were sent by the patriotic sons and daughters of Kentucky, began to reach the army. The gratitude of the troops generally was beyond expression. Some had withstood the keen blasts of that cold northern country, until sometime in January, with linen hunting shirts and pantaloons, and many almost without either shoes or socks. General Payne in a letter to Governor Shelby, in which he expresses his gratitude, as well as that of the troops, says—

> As an *earnest* of her disposition to aid the National Government, Kentucky, at an early period, with a characteristic ardour, sent forth more than her quota required by the government; and whilst a spark of genuine feeling animates the breasts of her volunteers in the North-Western Army, they can never cease to feel a lively gratitude for the further *earnest* of her anxiety for the cause, manifested in the late abundant supply of clothing.

It certainly was a source of heartfelt satisfaction, to express a proper sense of the obligations under which the patriotism of the *sons* of Kentucky had placed her volunteers; but the pleasure was greatly heightened when we reflected that to the *daughters* of Kentucky we were mostly indebted for imperious supplies to meet the blasts of a northern winter.

I hope it is not still too late (though many who engaged in that laudable work have gone from this scene of war and bloodshed,) for me to express my unfeigned gratitude to the daughters of my native State for the blessings bestowed on me as an individual; and as I have never had an opportunity before to express myself, permit me further to say, that these favors, while I possess a spark of feeling, shall never cease to produce a lively sense of gratitude. Help, in real need, is not forgotten.

On the day of our arrival a recent Indian camp was discovered about one half mile from us. Captain Williams was immediately despatched, with twenty five men, to pursue the Indians. He very soon overtook and routed them. A few shots were exchanged, by which some on both sides were wounded.

A large storehouse was immediately commenced for the purpose of securing the provisions and baggage. We found a quantity of corn in the fields, which was soon gathered; and before any machinery was prepared to pound and sift it, a quantity was boiled whole, and eaten without even salt. But we quickly arranged to have it made into hominy, and after the hogs came, we fared well upon "hog and hominy." You may judge of our relish for our food, when I tell you that one of our company, whose name I will not give, eat so much corn that he appeared to be actually foundered, and unable to walk for more than a week.

On the evening of the thirteenth, two Frenchmen arrived from the River Raisin with information that the Indians routed by Captain Williams had passed that place on their way to Malden, carrying with them intelligence of our advance. They said the Indians had threatened to kill their inhabitants and burn their town, and begged for protection from the American arms. They were charged with a despatch from Mr. Day, a citizen who was friendly to our cause, and who stated that the British were seizing all suspected persons at the River Raisin, and confining them at Malden prison, and were preparing to carry off all provisions of every description.

On the *fourteenth* another messenger arrived, and on the *sixteenth* two more came in. They all confirmed the news brought by the first, and solicited protection, as they were afraid the people would be massacred and the town burned by the Indians whenever our army should advance upon them. They stated the present force of the enemy to be two companies of Canadians, and about two hundred Indians, but that more Indians might be expected to assemble. The greatest anxiety now prevailed in our army to advance in force sufficient to defeat the enemy at that place. A council of officers was called by the general, a majority of whom were decidedly in favour of sending a strong detachment—Colonel Allen supported that side of the question with ardour.

On the morning of the seventeenth, Colonel Lewis, with five hundred and fifty men, took up their line of march for the River Raisin. The same day Colonel Allen followed with one hundred and ten more, who came up with Lewis late in the evening, where he was encamped at Presque Isle, Early on the morning of the same day General Winchester prepared a despatch to inform General Harrison of this movement. He stated that his principal object was to prevent the flour and grain from being carried off by the enemy; that if he got possession of Frenchtown he intended to hold it, and that a co-operating reinforcement from the right wing might be necessary.

Before the express had started with this letter, information was received from Colonel Lewis at Presque Isle, a distance of twenty miles in advance, that there were four hundred Indians at the River Raisin, and that Colonel Elliott was expected from Malden, with a detachment to attack the camp at the Rapids. Colonel Lewis set out very early next morning, intending, if possible, to anticipate Colonel Elliott at Frenchtown. That village lies midway between Presque Isle and Malden, the distance to each being eighteen miles. The most of our march was on the ice on Miami Bay, and the borders of Lake Erie. When we had arrived within a few miles of the River Raisin we were discovered by some Indians, who hastened to give the alarm to the main body of the enemy.

Before we left the border of the lake, a halt was called to take some refreshment. Having resumed our march, a piece of timbered land was passed through, and as the troops proceeded in the open plain they were formed into three lines, each corps being in the proper place for action. The right was commanded by Colonel Allen, and was composed of the companies of Captains McCracken, Bledsoe, and Matson. I was in Captain Bledsoe's company during this expedition. The left wing was commanded by Major Graves, and was composed of the companies of Hamilton, Williams, and Kelly. The centre consisted of the companies of Hightower, Collier, and Sabree, and was commanded by Major Madison. The advance guard consisted of the companies of Captains Hickman, Graves, and Jones, under the command of Captain Ballard, acting as major.

When we arrived within a quarter of a mile of the village, and discovered the enemy in motion, the line of battle was formed— expecting an immediate attack—but it was soon perceived the enemy did not intend to risk a combat in the open field. The detachment broke off by the right of companies and marched under the fire of the enemy's cannon until we arrived on the river. We succeeded well in crossing, though the ice in many places was very slippery. Having crossed, instantly the long roll was beat (the signal for a general charge.) Majors Graves and Madison were ordered to possess themselves of the houses and picketing, about which the enemy had collected, and where they had placed their cannon.

This order was promptly executed, and both battalions advanced under an incessant shower of bullets; neither the picketing nor fencing over which they passed retarded their progress or success, for the enemy in that quarter was dislodged.—meantime, Colonel Allen fell in with them a considerable distance to the right, when, after pursuing them to the woods, they made a stand with their howitzer and small arms, covered by a chain of inclosed lots and a group of houses, having in their rear a thick brushy wood filled with fallen timber. Orders were now given through Major Garrard to Majors Graves and Madison to possess themselves of the woods on the left, and move up towards the main body of the enemy as fast as practicable, and divert their attention from Colonel Allen.

At the moment the fire commenced with the battalions, the right wing advanced, and the enemy was soon driven from the fencing and houses, and our troops began to enter the woods in close pursuit. The fight now became very close, and extremely hot on the right wing— the enemy concentrating the chief of their forces of both kinds to force the lines, but still kept moving in a retreat, although slowly, for we were much exhausted. The joint exertions of Graves, Madison, and Allen, were successful in completely routing the enemy. The distance they retreated before us was not less than *two* miles, and every foot of the way under charge. The battle lasted from three o'clock until dark! The detachment was then drawn off in good order, and encamped upon the ground the enemy first occupied. About the going down of the sun, I received a wound in my right shoulder. A moment before I received the shot, I saw John Locke and Joseph Simpson advancing together, some distance to the left, and ahead of the main body. One was killed and the other wounded not far from the spot where I last

27

saw them.

Colonel Lewis says:

> The gallant conduct of Colonel Allen during every charge of this warmly contested action, has raised for him no ordinary military merit. Majors Graves and Madison deserve high praise for their undeviating attention to orders, and the energy and despatch with which they executed them. Captain Blan B. Ballard also led the van with great skill and bravery.
>
> I take this opportunity of tendering my most hearty thanks to Brigade Major Garrard, Captain Smith, and Adjutant McCuller, who acted as my aids, for the great support they gave me during the whole of the action. The company officers acted with great bravery.
>
> Both officers and soldiers supported the double character of Americans and Kentuckians.

It was impossible for us to ascertain the exact force of the enemy; but from the best information, there were about *one* hundred British and *four* hundred Indians. It was said Major Reynolds was present and commanded the whole. Their number killed we could not ascertain, and perhaps it is unknown to the Americans until the present time. From the number found on the field where the battle commenced, and from the blood and trails where they had dragged off their dead and wounded, the slaughter must have been considerable. One Indian and two Canadian militia were taken prisoners. So steady and composed were our men in the assaults, that while the enemy were killed or driven from their houses, not a woman or child was injured. Our loss was *twelve* killed and fifty five wounded. Joseph Simpson was the only man belonging to Captain Simpson's company that was killed in the first engagement.

Very few of our men were killed or wounded until we reached the woods; here we fought under great disadvantages, not being acquainted with the ground, and most of us being unacquainted with the Indian mode of warfare. Thus our want of experience and eagerness to overtake the enemy, gave them a decided advantage over us. Their method was to retreat rapidly until they were out of sight, (which was soon the case in the brushy woods,) and while we were advancing they were preparing to give us another fire; so we were generally under the necessity of firing upon them as they were retreating. During the charge, I saw several of our brave boys lying upon the snow wallowing in the agonies of death. But none could stop even to help his brother, for our situation required the utmost exertion of every man as long as he could render any service.

It was sometime after dark before we reached the place from which we drove the enemy, where we encamped for the night, and where we were accommodated with all the necessaries of life, and every attention which our situation required. I cannot but speak a word in favour of our physicians: too much cannot be said in their praise for the prompt attention which they gave on that occasion. Though it was late before the houses were prepared, and other arrangements made for the accommodation of the wounded, yet every man had his wounds dressed before the surgeons took any rest. Their memory deserves to be perpetuated.

Immediately after the battle an express was sent to convey the news of our success to General Winchester, at whose camp he arrived before daylight; and from that place another was sent to communicate the intelligence to General Harrison.

Colonel Lewis was determined, if possible, to hold the place until a reinforcement could be sent on. We knew our situation was very critical, being only *eighteen* miles from Malden; yet it appeared to make scarcely any impression upon our minds, so long had we been in the region of the enemy, and so much had we suffered from cold, hunger, and fatigue. The fare was now so different to what we had been accustomed since we left the settlement in Ohio—and some of the troops were so much elated with having driven the enemy from their fortifications, and having taken possession of their provisions, &c.—that we almost seemed to forget that we had an enemy in the world.

On the evening of the nineteenth, General Winchester left the Rapids with two hundred and fifty men, which were all that could be spared from that post. He reached us on the night of the twentieth, and encamped in an open lot on the right of the former detachment. Colonel Lewis had encamped in a place where he was defended by garden pickets, which were sufficient to defend from an attack of small arms. Colonel Wells commanded the reinforcement; and to him the general named, but did not positively command, a breast-work for the protection of his camp. The general himself, established his quarters in a house upon the south side of the river; about three hundred yards from the camp.

On the 21st, a place was selected for the whole detachment to encamp, in good order, with a determination to fortify the next day.

About sunset Colonel —— solicited and obtained leave to return to the rapids. On this day, certain information was obtained that the British were preparing for an attack, and that we might look for it in a very short time. A Frenchman came from Malden with information that a large force of British and Indians—which he supposed would number near three thousand—were about to march from that place shortly after he left it. But even this was not credited, or if believed, was little regarded by many of the troops! The most of the men acted as though they knew themselves to be perfectly secure; some wandering; about the town until a late hour at night! For myself, I can say, I felt little dread, though I had reason to believe that our situation was very perilous. I slept soundly until awaked by the startling cry of "to arms! to arms!" and the thundering of cannon and roar of small arms, and the more terrific yelling of savages.

Major Madison and Colonel Lewis, together with most of the officers, had cautioned their men to be on their guard, and be prepared for an attack. Guards, as usual, were placed out; but as it was extremely cold, no picket guard was placed upon the road by which the enemy was expected to advance. At daybreak, on the morning of the 22nd, just as the drum began to beat, three guns were fired by the sentinels; in an instant the men were at their posts. The British now began to open a heavy fire of cannon and small arms. They appeared mostly to direct their cannon to the house which contained the ammunition, and where the wounded officers lay. Every circumstance attending this awful scene, conspired to make it more alarming—the time and manner in which it was commenced—for they approached in the dark with profound silence—not a breath was heard until all was ready, then, sudden as a flash of powder, the bloody work began.

The first thing that presented itself to my sight, after awaking out of sleep and going to the window, was the fiery tail of a bombshell—and these came in quick succession. Just at this moment, the fire of small arms from both sides began. For a considerable time it was one continued roar. But I could, nevertheless, distinguish between the enemies guns and our own. The British regulars approached immediately in front of Colonel Lewis' detachment, but did not long remain within the reach of small arms, for a well directed fire from the pickets soon repulsed them, with the loss of a number of their soldiers whom they left upon the field. They would not have approached so near if they had known precisely our situation. They told me whilst I was at Detroit, that they thought we were encamped in the open field outside of the garden pickets; but as soon as it was light, and they discovered their mistake, they retreated. The yelling of the Indians appeared to be mostly on the right, though some was heard upon the left, but none in the centre.

The reinforcement which had arrived with General Winchester, and which was unprotected by any breastwork, after maintaining the conflict for a short time, was overpowered and fell back. Just at this time General Winchester came up and ordered the retreating troops to rally and form behind the second bank of the river, and inclining toward the centre, take refuge behind the picketing. These orders were probably not heard, and being hard pressed both by the British and Indians in front and on their right flank, they were completely thrown into confusion, and retreated in disorder over the river. A detachment which was sent from the pickets to reinforce the right wing, and a few others who supposed the whole army was ordered to retreat, joined in its flight. Those brave men, Colonels Allen and Lewis, both followed, hoping to assist in rallying the troops.

An attempt was made to rally them on the south side of the river, behind the houses and garden pickets, but all in vain; the Indians had taken possession of the woods behind them, and thus completely cut off their retreat, and no alternative now remained but to stand and fight a superior force, which was every moment accumulating, and which had every advantage, or to retreat to better ground. In their dismay and confusion they attempted to pass a narrow lane—the Indians were on both sides, and shot them in every direction. A large party which had gained the woods on the right, were surrounded and massacred without distinction.

Captain Matson, who was an eyewitness, states:

After crossing the river, they attempted to form and give battle, but the houses being in the way, they failed in the attempt. They then retreated through a lane for one hundred yards, on the sides of which a number of Indians were placed, who injured them very much.

He, though wounded, joined in the retreat. He further states:

The Indians pursued on each side for about one mile, they then fell back in the rear.

He then saw Colonel Lewis and requested him to form the men and make a stand against the Indians once more, as many of the men

31

were wounded and could retreat no farther. The attempt was made without success, as many were without arms. He afterwards saw General Winchester, and begged of him for God's sake to make a stand, as the Indians were in close pursuit, and he himself was much exhausted, and was convinced that many more were in the same condition. The general informed him that the men could not be rallied.

After retreating about three miles from Raisin they came to a field, those on foot passed through, and those on horseback rode around. Here Captain Matson, General Winchester, Colonel Lewis, Doctor Ervine and Doctor Patrick, were seen going slowly forward, their horses much fatigued, and a number of Indians pursuing on fresh horses, who soon overtook them.

Captain Matson, seeing the Indians within one hundred yards of him, slipped through a fence, pulled off his shoes, ran along the fence in a stooping position about sixty yards, and hid himself in some high grass. The Indians continued to pursue those who were before. He thinks there were not more than fifty men ahead of him. After the Indians had passed by, the captain moved to a prairie, where he concealed himself until dark, and then pushed on to the Rapids, keeping the road a distance to the right.

Mr. Newel, one of Captain Matson's company, concealed himself in a barn, near to where the Indians returned. His account is, that they had "a number of scalps tied to their saddles, and a number also of our men tied." He left the barn on the 23rd at night—lost his way, and went back to the River Raisin in the night. He was there informed that all who stood their ground had been taken prisoners, and that but few had been killed. It is due to the memory of Doctor Davis to notice a circumstance which was related by one of the wounded. He stated, that at the commencement of the action he took a gun belonging to a companion of his, also wounded, and moved forward to join the company; the doctor seeing him, said, "give me the gun, your situation will not allow you to expose yourself," and went himself into the engagement—showing his promptness in every part of duty, whether in dressing the wounded, or in facing the enemy as a private soldier.

I made inquiry of all the prisoners which I could see, about Colonel Allen and Captain Simpson, but could hear nothing satisfactory. I spent a year in prison with several men who were in the retreating party, and often heard them relate what they knew of that sad affair; but as they did not belong to our company, and were not personally acquainted with Colonel Allen and Captain Simpson, and as they

were in such a state of alarm—all around being dismay and confusion—they could not particularly notice any person, but directed their
whole attention toward their own personal safety. Perhaps the whole
truth relating to those brave men, who fell in the retreating party, will
never be known. It has been related that Captain Simpson fell not far
from the mouth of the lane through which the troops had just passed.
It has also been stated of Colonel Allen:

> After making several unsuccessful efforts to rally his men—
> entreating them to halt, and to sell their lives as dearly as pos-
> sible—that he had retreated about two miles, until he was ex-
> hausted; he then sat down upon a log and resigned himself up
> to his fate. An Indian chief perceiving him to be an officer of
> distinction, was anxious to make him a prisoner. As soon as he
> came to the colonel, he threw his gun across his lap and told
> him in Indian to surrender and he should be safe. Another sav-
> age having advanced with a hostile appearance, Colonel Allen,
> with one stroke of his sword, laid him dead at his feet. A third
> Indian had the honour of shooting one of the first and bravest
> men of Kentucky.

Before we leave the retreating party, it may not be out of place to
record two circumstances which show the estimate which the Indians set upon bravery, and also how they treat cowardice. The circumstances were related to me as follows: A young man after the Indians
had taken him prisoner, and appeared inclined to save his life, showed
great alarm, and at length told the Indians that he would tell them
where they might find a great many white men, and might kill them
all, &c. The Indians instantly took his life, although until then they
had showed no hostility toward him. The other related to the narra-
tor himself. He stated that after the Indians took him prisoner, they
marched him very hard, until he became so much exhausted that he
was no longer able to travel as fast as they wished him to go. They
shook their tomahawks at him, and told him that he must march faster
or die.

He was starving and sick, but he kept on as fast and as far as he
could, and when he could go no farther he laid down upon the ground
and told them to kill him. They motioned with their weapons as if
they intended to take his life, but when they saw his resolution they
became attached to him, and aided him all they could to go on the
journey, and were kind to him as long as he remained with them.

After the British had withdrawn their forces from our front, and the Indians had mostly disappeared, and the firing, save a few scattering guns from some scouting Indians, had ceased, the situation of the retreating party became a matter of anxious concern with Colonel Lewis' detachment, which was left within the picketing. Some were heard to express their fears that they were generally cut off, because of the firing heard in that direction. During all the time the troops within the pickets stood to their posts, and now in this critical moment fully sustained the character of brave Kentuckians. Majors Madison and Garrard, when the ammunition grew short in the cartridge boxes, were employed busily to furnish the men with a supply, carrying them around in their pocket handkerchiefs and strewing them upon the ground at the soldiers' feet, and at the same time exhorting them never to think of a surrender. Some of our brave men fell by a party of savages coming up under the north bank of the river. From the house containing the wounded, they were discovered. Information was given immediately, and by a detachment they were soon routed.

The firing now had ceased, except a shot as an Indian was seen passing about. The men had to keep a strict look out to prevent surprise, as the Indians were skulking about, and no one felt safe for a single moment. After the cannon, which had been placed down the river about two hundred yards, had ceased firing—the horse and driver which supplied the ammunition being killed—those of us who had received wounds in the battle (myself among the rest,) proceeded to take our breakfasts of a little light bread. This was all that we could now procure.

All the while we were at a loss to know why the British troops had been withdrawn to the woods, and the Indians left alone to contend by themselves; but we afterwards learned that they were waiting the return of the Indians who had pursued the retreating party. When they returned they brought General Winchester and Colonel Lewis with them.

As soon as General Proctor, the British commander, heard that General Winchester was taken, he basely determined to take advantage of it, and thereby procure the surrender of all those within the picketing. He represented to the general that nothing but an immediate surrender could save the Americans from an indiscriminate Indian massacre. It was not until the flag approached, borne by Major Overton, one of the generals' aids, bringing orders from General Winchester to surrender, that we dreamed that the general, or Colonel Lewis, were prisoners. When this news reached the troops, that General Winchester had surrendered the whole as prisoners to the British, it was like a shock of lightning from one end of the lines to the other.

A number declared that they never would submit, let the consequences be what they might. But when they found that Majors Madison and Garrard had consented to obey the orders of General Winchester, some of them, in great rage, threw down their guns with such force as: to shiver the stocks from the barrels.

When the flag above named was first discovered to advance, various conjectures were entertained of the design. The greater number supposed that the enemy was tired of the game and wished to quit, and desired permission to bury their dead, which were not few. There were also many badly wounded. It was plain to discover where their lines had been formed, by the number of killed and wounded still lying on the field.

When Major Madison approached the flag, Colonel Proctor, with great haughtiness, demanded an immediate surrender, or he would set the town on fire, and that the Indians should not be restrained from committing an indiscriminate massacre. Major Madison observed "that it had been customary for the Indians to massacre the wounded prisoners after a surrender," and "that he could not agree to any capitulation which General Winchester might direct, unless the safety and protection of his men were secured."

Colonel Proctor then said, "Sir, do you mean to dictate for me?"

"No," replied Madison, "I mean to dictate for *myself*—and we prefer to sell our lives as dearly as possible, rather than be massacred in cold blood."

Proctor then agreed to receive a surrender upon the terms, that all private property should be respected—that sleds should be sent next morning to remove the sick and wounded to Amherstburg—and that in the mean time they should be protected by a guard, and the side arms should be restored to the officers at Malden.

But this unprincipled deceiver, bearing the title of general, suffered the savages to violate the treaty before his own eyes. Whilst the men were in parade to surrender their arms in order, the Indians began to tear up the tents and to plunder in every direction gathering up everything in the shape of clothing, and every knapsack which they could find. I could not bear arms from my wound, and whilst the men were on parade, some time before they were marched off, I was passing about and noticing the movements and work of the Indians. They were striving who should get the most plunder. I passed around to the front of the house to take a look at the boys before they left us; they braved it off as well as might have been expected. Some looked a little dejected—others joked and laughed. One, who had not yet fallen into the ranks, was standing upon a stile-block, and said to the English: "Well, you have taken the greatest set of game cocks that ever came from Kentuck." I wish I could remember his name—he was calculated to remind one of a game cock.

John Locke and Jesse Fisher, of our company, were badly wounded; and as both Proctor and Elliott had promised to send sleds for us in the morning, and though able to walk myself, I resolved to risk it, and stay and assist those who were not able to help themselves. Captain Hart, of Lexington, Kentucky, expressed great anxiety to be taken with the prisoners to Malden. His men offered to carry him, and were reluctant to leave him behind; but Colonel Elliott, the commander of the Indians, being well acquainted with Hart and his family—having in former life received great fevers from them in Kentucky—assured him that he need not be under the least apprehension of danger—that the Indians would not molest those that were left—and that, upon the honour of a soldier, he would send his own sleigh for him on the next morning and have him conveyed to Malden.

Some of the more discerning apprehended great danger in being left, and insisted on all that could go to do so. The brave Captain Hickman saw the danger, and desired all that could walk not to remain; for, said he to Mr. Holton, (now Captain Holton,) "there are more of us here now than will ever get away." This, from what I could afterwards learn, was the sentiment entertained and expressed by all the officers. But what could they do in their wounded and defenceless condition, being no doubt doomed to death by the infamous Proctor and Elliott.

These brave officers and soldiers, who had battled against the very elements for months, and had passed through sufferings almost equal to death itself, lived through it all only to meet the most horrid of all deaths—of being butchered in cold blood, and that without having the power or means of defence.

The parting was a solemn one, and not only solemn, but in reference to most of those unhappy victims, it was final. Many were greatly affected, especially the friends of Hart and Hickman. But having fallen into the hands of a bloody and heartless tyrant, this brave "Spartan band" were compelled to submit to his cruel dictates.

No time was now to be lost—all eyes were directed towards the Rapids—the cowardly Proctor dreaded the approach of General Harrison, and therefore made all possible speed to get out of his way, fearing to meet so brave and experienced an officer; and well he might, for the sight of General Harrison at that time would have been death to the hopes and prospects of these red and white savages, while it would have been a jubilee to those hapless Kentuckians who were doomed to death.

After a few formalities of delivering up arms, &c., they were hurried off and driven like so many beasts to market, but with much less tenderness and kindness than a merciful man would show to his beast. After their arrival at Malden, they were crowded into a pen, and there guarded, without anything to protect them from the weather. Their bread, what little they got, was thrown to them like throwing corn to swine.

Though there was a much shorter rout by which the prisoners might have been returned to their own country, yet this did not satisfy these wanton tyrants—nothing would do but the prisoners must, in the dead of winter, march on foot up Detroit River; thence up the Thames, to Delaware town; thence across the country to Burlington Heights; and from this point to Fort Niagara—a distance perhaps of five hundred miles—when the whole could have been accomplished in about two days' march, by sending them back to the rapids, where they would have fallen in with their friends at once. But no,—nothing but the infliction of suffering would satisfy those cruel tyrants.

These things are but barely mentioned, that the attention of the young and rising generation may be led to reflect upon them. And that they may have some knowledge of what their fathers suffered in defence of the liberties they now so richly enjoy.

After the men were marched off. Everything was quiet; now and then an Indian was seen straying about as though seeking plunder. They did not manifest hostility, and our fears began to subside, and we hoped to be conveyed to the army on the next morning.

Doctors Todd and Bowers were left to take care of the wounded. Major Reynolds and three interpreters composed the only guard to protect the wounded from the savages. We were hoping that General Harrison, then on his way from the Rapids, would just at that time arrive and give us relief by his reinforcement. Major Reynolds was evidently uneasy lest Harrison should arrive. Some of the Indians staid in town until late in the night. Major Reynolds and the interpreters left some time in the night; at least they left our house, and we saw them no more.

As night came on, our fears began to increase. An Indian came into the house and told us that he thought there was danger to be feared from some Indians, which he thought were disposed to do mischief. He manifested some uneasiness himself; perhaps fearing that some Indian might shoot into the house. He appeared to be well acquainted with the affairs of the Indians, in general, and had some knowledge of the movements and designs of the British and American Armies— which he was not at all backward in expressing. He spoke the English language fluently; and from his manners, I would infer that he had spent much of his life with the white population. His principal object seems to have been to gain all the information possible about General Harrison, and the strength of the North-Western army.

It is probable, however, that another object of his visit was to find out from us whether we thought it probable that General Harrison would advance immediately with the main body of his army to make an attack upon Malden. He gained but little information from us. There was but one man of our company thoughtless enough to give any *correct* information, whose name I shall not mention. He told us many things about Tecumseh and the Indians from the north that were coming to join them in the spring. He seemed to entertain no doubt but that they would, when all their forces were brought together, find it an easy matter to conquer all the armies the United States could send to the north. After remaining in our room about two hours, he very politely bid us goodnight, and left us.

After the departure of this Indian chief, (for I have but little doubt but what he was among the principal leaders of the Indian forces,) some conversation ensued among ourselves in reference to the designs of this crafty and intelligent chief.

There was, as well as I can recollect, but one opinion expressed on the subject; and I believe it was the opinion of all, that that would be the last night with most of us. We dreaded an attack during the night; for this Indian, just as he left, said "I am afraid some of the mischievous boys will do some mischief before morning." After remaining in this state of suspense for more than an hour, expecting every moment that the savages would come rushing upon us; but everything becoming quiet, we laid down upon our blankets to rest: but rested very little during this dismal night. Dreadful as was the night, the morning was more fearful. Just as the sun had risen upon us, and our hopes began to rise; and just as we were about to eat the morsel of bread left us by our friends who had been marched off the day before, that we might be ready at a moment's warning to leave, should the British send sleighs for us, we heard a noise in the passage, and before we had time to think, the door of our room was forced open by an Indian, who entered with tomahawk in hand, ready to commence his bloody work. He was quickly followed by others.

Their first object was plunder. They had no sooner entered the door of our room, than they began, in the most cruel manner, to strip the blankets and clothes off the wounded as they lay upon the floor. Fortunately for me, I was at the opposite side of the room from the door at which the Indians entered, near a door leading into the front room of the house; and finding there was no time to lose, I immediately passed out into the front room, where I met one of the most savage looking Indians I ever beheld. His very appearance was enough to terrify the stoutest heart. His face painted as black as charcoal could make it, plainly indicative of his deadly design; a bunch of long feathers fastened on his head, almost as large as a half bushel; a large tomahawk, the instrument of death, in his right hand; a scalping knife fastened to his belt. He instantly seized me by the collar, and led me out at the front door.

At first I manifested some unwillingness to go with him. He then spoke very earnestly in his own language, and at the same time pulled me along forcibly, as if to remove me from the scene of death within. He led me through the front gate, and down the river about one hundred yards to the other houses, in which were Captains Hart, Hickman, and others. After leading me through the front gate, he left me. Just at this time, Captain Hart came out of his room, barefooted, with nothing on but shirt and drawers. In this condition he stood in the snow for some length of time pleading for his life. I here met with the chief who had been in our room in the evening.

Captain Hart understanding the designs of Proctor and Elliott, and knowing that the only possible chance for life, under the circumstances, was to make some arrangement with the Indians. For this purpose he sought an interview with this one, as he seemed to be a leader, and very intelligent. They met in the front yard, near the gate, about the time I came in.

I stood by and heard the conversation. Captain Hart's first remark, if I mistake not, was, that he was an acquaintance of Colonel Elliott's, and that he (Elliott) had promised to send his own sleigh for him.

The Indian replied, "Elliott has deceived you—he does not intend to fulfil his promise."

Well, said Captain Hart, "if you will agree to take me, I will give you a horse, or a hundred dollars. You shall have it on our arrival at Malden."

The Indian said, "I cannot take you."

"Why?" asked Captain Hart.

"You are too badly wounded," said the Indian.

Captain Hart then asked the Indian, what they intended to do with them?

"Boys," said the Indian, raising himself up into an attitude and air of consequence and insult, "*your are all to be killed*."

Though involved in the same calamity myself, I could but notice the calmness and composure with which the brave officer received the sentence of death. The only reply which I heard him make was in the language of prayer to Almighty God to sustain him in this hour of trial. Feeling that the awful sentence included myself as well as all the rest, my heart seemed to sink within me, expecting every moment to receive the fatal blow. Just at this moment an Indian dragged Captain Hickman out of the house by one arm, and threw him down near where I stood, with his face on the snow. He was tomahawked, but not yet dead. He lay strangling in his blood.

From this scene I turned away, and walking round the end of the house, towards the back yard, met an Indian at the corner of the house, who took hold of me and searched my pockets for money, but finding none, passed on. I then passed on round the house, leaving the main building on my right, and walking slowly that I might not appear to have any design, and that I might not attract the attention of the enemy. I thought, possibly, I might reach a small log building which I discovered not far from the house. As there was but one small entrance into it, and as it appeared dark within, it seemed to present the only possible refuge; and as there was no time to lose, and as life and death were depending, I determined to make the attempt to gain this place of retreat.

But as I was within a few paces of my hiding place, an Indian coming from the opposite direction met me, and taking hold of me, asked me where I was wounded: I placed my hand upon my shoulder. He then felt of it, and finding that the wound was not bad, he took me back to the house where he had deposited his plunder; put a blanket around me, gave me a hat, then took me to the back door of the house in which the wounded lay, and gave me his gun and plunder in charge. In a moment everything seemed to wear a different aspect. I now experienced one of those sudden transitions of mind impossible to be either conceived or expressed, except by those whose unhappy lot it has been, to be placed in like circumstances. Until now, despair had spread its gloomy mantle over me; but hope, that cheering companion, again visited my sinking heart, and I again saw a faint prospect that my life *might* be spared.

Thus situated, I had time to see what was passing around me. I had command of the way leading to Malden; and I saw but one road. I remained in this position about two hours, during which time I saw several pass—I suppose all who were able. Here I saw a striking example of the estimate a man places on life. I saw some of our own company—old acquaintances who were so badly wounded that they could scarcely be moved in their beds, understanding that those who could not travel on foot to Malden were all to be tomahawked, pass on their way to Malden, hobbling along on sticks. Poor fellows, they were soon overtaken by their merciless enemies and inhumanly butchered.

A few moments after, being placed here by the Indian who claimed me, another Indian set fire to the house. The fire was built in the passage near the backdoor where I stood. After the fire had taken considerable hold of the house, an Indian came running downstairs with a keg of powder in his hand, with the head out. Just as he got to the foot of the stairs his foot slipped, and he come very near falling into the fire with the powder. Had the powder caught, both he and I would have perished.

The general opinion, I believe is, in reference to Captain Hart, that an Indian engaged to take him to Malden; and that another Indian, unwilling that he should go, shot him on the road. This may be true, but has always appeared to me improbable. From the position I occupied, having command of the way to Malden, I believe I saw all who passed in that direction, but saw nothing of Captain Hart. Upon the whole, I am induced to think that Captain Hart met his fate in the front yard where I left him.

I remained here until the roof of the house set on fire had fallen in. I heard no cry within, from which I inferred that the wounded were killed before the house was burnt.

My Indian finally returned, bringing with him one of the United States' pack horses; and placing his bundle of plunder on him, gave me the bridle, making signs to march on towards Malden. I soon found the bodies of those poor hapless boys who had made the attempt, but were too badly wounded to travel, massacred, scalped, and stripped. When we reached the woods, we halted a short time by the fire. We then went on to Stony Creek, where the British had encamped the night before the battle. Their wounded were still there, waiting to be conveyed to Malden.

Here the Indians made a large fire of rails, and gave the prisoners some bread. Our number was eight or ten. As we were eating, one of the Indians deliberately walked up to his prisoner, a fine looking young man, a son of Dr. Blythe of Lexington, and struck the tomahawk into his head. I was looking the young man in the face when he received the deadly blow; he closed his eyes, and sunk under the first stroke of the deadly weapon. After he had fallen, and received two or three strokes from the hand of the Indian, an old Frenchman took the weapon out of the hand of the savage and gave the dying man another stroke upon the head, which stilled him in death. (See note following).

★★★★★★

Note:—Having marked the place where this old Frenchman lived, in order that I might the more readily find him, should I ever be permitted to visit the country again: and having taken particular notice of the house, I found no difficulty in ascertaining its location, and even the very habitation in which the old Tory resided.

After the lapse of about eighteen months, from the time I was there a prisoner with the Indians, I was there again under General McArthur, who commanded a regiment of mounted volunteers—one battalion of which was from Kentucky, under the command of Major Peter Dudley.

Passing by this old man's house, in company with Benjamin Whitaker, our lieutenant, we met this man in the street near his own house; I immediately recognized him as the individual who had so inhumanly assisted in the massacre of young Mr. Blythe, at Stony Creek.

I mentioned the circumstance to Whitaker, and asked his advice in reference to the course best to be pursued; who instantly replied, "*let us take him.*"

I was glad of the opportunity, and forthwith approached him, and the first salutation, as near as I can recollect, was, "*Well sir, do you know anything of me?*"

His reply was, "No sir, I know nothing about you."

"Well sir," said I, "I know you very well."

He seemed at first to be somewhat surprised at my confident address, and looking on me very earnestly seemed to express some doubts on the subject. I, however, soon removed the old man's doubts, by remarking to him, "You are the man who was guilty of the cruel and inhuman act of assisting the savages in killing one of the prisoners at Stony Creek, taken at Raisin, January 23, 1813. You are the very man, sir, and I saw you do it." These words come upon him, no doubt, very unexpectedly; and being seconded by the voice of conscience within, made him tremble. He discovered evident marks of fear, his countenance grew pale in an instant; and finding that his very fear had betrayed him, he did not deny it; but offered as an excuse that the Indians required it of him, and that he was afraid to refuse. This excuse, however, did not satisfy us. We considered, that as a citizen of Detroit, he had no business with the British Army in time of battle. We, therefore, took him, without any further ceremony about it, and delivered him over to the proper authorities. He was confined in jail for eight or ten days, and then brought out for trial. I, of course, was the only evidence that appeared against him. He plead the same excuse he did when we first arrested him.

After nearly a whole day's managing in the matter, between the lawyers and the jury, and after alarming the old fellow nearly to death, they acquitted him.

I soon found that this circumstance had enraged the French population against me—particularly the old Catholic French. I, therefore, found it necessary, when going alone up town, to take my gun with me well loaded: this I considered a sufficient protection against any attack from that quarter.

★★★★★★

This greatly alarmed us. There appeared to be nothing in his case, that we could see, that made it necessary for him to die and not the rest of us. We now expected every moment to share the same barbarity. One of our company, a young man by the name of Jones, was so terrified that he began to weep, and moved to the opposite side of the fire, thinking that those nearest the danger would be the first victims. We urged him to be still, and not to discover such marks of fear, or that he would certainly be killed. The Indian who had taken me, and claimed me as his, was at this time a few steps from us, adjusting his pack; I stepped up to him, and asked him if they were going to kill us all. He answered "*yes*." I went back to the fire and tried to eat, as well as I could, without an appetite. It was now about two o'clock, p. m., and having eaten but little for three days past, and that day had taken nothing until we arrived at Stony Creek; but this awful cold-blooded butchery took away all desire for food. I soon saw that he did not understand my question, and I was then somewhat relieved. It has been said, and perhaps with due regard to truth, that many of the Indians engaged in this dreadful havoc, were under the influence of rum. They were supplied with it by the British, and when under its influence were more savage than savages.

We now took up our march towards Malden, leaving some of the Indians and their prisoners behind. Some of them I saw no more. They may have shared the same fate at the fire as the young man above. He was as able to travel as any of us, being only slightly wounded. He had no shoes—this may have been the reason why they did not take him on. We had gone but a short distance until we came to a number of Indians who were dancing the war dance around the fire. Here some of them had encamped on the night before the battle.

As soon as we arrived, I saw that the Indians were drunk. Here my fears were again alarmed—being in the midst of a savage camp—dancing the war dance—the blood of scores fresh upon them—and under the influence of strong drink! Whilst my Indian kept sober I had some hopes of protection. It was not long, however, until I saw him go into the dance and begin to drink. Now I almost yielded myself up to despair. As I stood holding his horse with a sad countenance, he came to me and gave me a roasted potato. He also made some expression of friendship, which once more tended to revive my drooping hopes.

The Indians having finished their dance, we proceeded towards Malden, and at night we encamped in the woods upon the snow. We took supper upon a piece cut from the side of a hog, boiled with the hair on, without bread and without salt. It rained during the night, and our situation was anything but agreeable; yet I felt thankful that it was no worse.

Many strange reflections rolled across my mind during the evening. The scenes of the day—such as I had never before witnessed—would occasionally force themselves upon my mind, the tendency of which was to spread a gloom upon everything around me, and to heighten my fears. We were in a dense forest, removed from the sight of any habitation of man, the snow about eighteen inches deep, the rain making it still more insupportable.

I kept my eyes upon the Indians, particularly the one to whom I belonged, watching every motion, every step, and expression of his countenance. As the shades of night began to close upon our gloomy retreat, it seemed to shed a double horror upon the scene. The sad and heart-chilling thought would, in spite of all the efforts I could make to frown it back, intrude itself upon me, that I had been saved from the massacre only to meet a more horrid fate—that the fire they had kindled was perhaps to serve the double purpose of cooking their supper and roasting me to death. Whenever any of the company would take his tomahawk in his hand, the thought would instantly spring up, now I am gone.

This, take it altogether, was among the most trying scenes through which I passed during my imprisonment; not that I was actually in more danger, but taking all the circumstances together—the place, the time, and being separated from my friends in suffering, and being thrown alone, and for the first time to be secluded from all but a few savages whose hands were yet stained with the blood of my countrymen, and not knowing the moment my own might be shed—produced emotions extremely distressing and trying.

After we had eaten, the Indians began to make preparations for lodging, by scraping away the snow and placing bark down upon which to spread their blankets; they suspended a blanket, by means of a few poles, so as to keep the rain out of our faces. After engaging themselves in conversation for some time, which they seemed to enjoy exceedingly, and which was occasionally accompanied with loud exultations, the proposition was made to retire for the night. My feelings now became indescribable. Strange as it may appear, I was apprehensive that after I fell asleep they would take that opportunity to despatch me; a death of this kind appeared to me the most dreadful of all others.

With these feelings, by their direction I lay down, and knowing that they were careful to save all articles of clothing, I tied up my head in my pocket handkerchief, hoping that this might be some protection, believing that they would not tomahawk me without removing it, which I supposed they could not do without awaking me. Thus I lay me down by the side, and under the same blanket, with the Indian who claimed me, with fearful apprehensions that I should never again see the light of the sun. But notwithstanding the cold, the snow and rain, and my perilous condition, such had been the excitement of the day that I was completely overcome, and very soon fell into a sound sleep, and slept sweetly until morning. The light of the morning was hailed with expressions of gratitude to a kind and merciful Providence which had shielded me through such a night. With the return of the day I had a return of hope that I should yet be spared.

Early next morning we started on through the snow, mud and water. We had but little to eat, and no opportunity to warm; my clothing was scant, and not sufficient to protect me against the weather. We fell in with several small companies of Indians, some on foot and others on horseback, none offering any violence or showing any hostility, but all appearing anxious to look at me and make inquiries. Occasionally we heard a gun on the right or left; but when we got into the vicinity of Malden the firing was almost incessant—it seemed that the whole face of the country was covered with Indians, rejoicing over a vanquished enemy. I again began to feel that my condition was exceedingly perilous, and that I was only spared from the tomahawk at Raisin, to be led to the slaughter at Malden. Though I did not at this time fear so much from the Indian that claimed me as his, yet I had much to fear from the enraged and drunken savages which were to be seen in every direction.

A short time before night, as we were passing an old house, a squaw came out crying, and commenced beating me with all her strength. She smote me on my wounded shoulder, and raised my temper. For a short time I cared but little whether I lived or died, I thought if this was to be my treatment whenever I met a squaw, that I might as well give up at once and die. This was, however, my first and last whipping from a female Indian. That night we lodged at the house of a Frenchman, whose family was very kind. We went forward again next morning, and that day we reached the home of this Indian.

But on our way, having to pass the vicinity of Detroit, the Indians called at the house of the old Frenchman who had stained his hands in the blood of young Mr. Blythe, at Stony Creek—(I have since learned that this was the name of the young man.) They held a long conversation which I could not understand, because they conversed in Indian. The Frenchman seemed to enter heartily into the spirit of rejoicing. They smoked together, and passed other Indian compliments, all of which I noticed particularly; and not only that, but marked the place, and promised myself that if opportunity should offer, to pay him for it.

From this point we left the main road, leaving Detroit to our right; we soon passed through a large Indian camp; just as we were entering, a company came in who had been at the battle at Raisin, bringing in their wounded in sleighs; the one which I saw appeared to be very badly wounded, and contrary to all Indian custom, or dignity of Indian character, was heard to groan. But notwithstanding his extreme pain, he cast a most savage look at me as the sleigh passed.

In passing this camp many Indians came to the door of their tents to look, particularly the young squaws. Under all the circumstances, passing through just as they were, returning from the bloody scene of Raisin, and also bringing in some badly, perhaps mortally, wounded, I had fearful apprehensions—I knew not what moment an enraged savage would take my life.

After leaving this camp—at which we made no stay—I felt greatly relieved, believing there was some hope that we might pass safely on to our place of destination. As well as I recollect, we passed but very few Indians after this; but about sunset, when within a short distance of our Indian home, in passing over a pond on the ice, which at that time was covered with snow, the horse slipped and fell, but after some difficulty we succeeded in getting him on his feet again, and soon reached the vicinity of camp, which was announced to me by the Indian commencing the war-whoop at the top of his voice, which was responded to by a number of voices as loud and terrible as his own. All seemed to understand it—it was the sound of victory. As soon as we approached near enough to be recognized, every Indian, male and female, were out—all eyes directed towards us—and every man and boy shouted to the extent of their ability.

My feelings by this time—having recently witnessed so many scenes of blood, and having passed through so many hair-breadth escapes myself—had become almost deadened; but upon the approach of this camp, amid the shouts of savages, and not knowing for what purpose I should be brought there, unless to be a victim of sport for them, I *felt*, and this is all that I can say—for to express *what* I felt, I find to be impossible.

Here we found the home of his wife, and her father and mother, who all seemed glad to see us. The old squaw took me by the hand and led me into the hut, and gave me something to eat, which was in place. I now began to feel that I had friends in this family, and considered myself pretty safe. We spent about two weeks at this place, a few miles west of Detroit. A day or two before we left this encampment the Indians determined on having a spree. They went to Detroit and traded for a keg of rum. They had not been at home long until most of the men were drunk. I now again felt myself in danger, for one of them attempted to take my life; I escaped because he was drunk and could not get to me. That night the squaws hid me out in the woods behind a log in the snow. They made me a bed of hay, and covered me with their blankets.

When I awaked in the morning the frolic was all over. The Indians were lying about round the fires like hounds after a hard chase; the whiskey was dying in them, and they were sleepy and sick. The Indians now made ready to go out to their hunting ground; and after a few days' preparation we started. As well as I am able to judge, we travelled a west course. We were upon the road about two weeks; our sufferings were great from the intense cold, and from hunger; we had nothing to eat but what the hunters could kill by the way. I rendered what assistance I could in catching raccoons and porcupines, for these were our principal living whilst on the road. I suppose we travelled one hundred and fifty miles before we reached our destination. We now began to fare a little better, though we sometimes still suffered with hunger—it was either a *feast* or a *famine* with us. The Indians would eat up all the provisions with as much despatch as possible, and let every day provide for itself. Thus we spent our time for several weeks.

Here I will give an account of a very aged man who I saw on our way out to this place. There were many families on the way at the same time—not only their wives and children, but their young men. This caused me to think that they did not expect any more war during the winter season. It seemed that when their actual services were not necessary, they were then left to shift for themselves. This was in perfect character with all the doings of the British during this war. We had been travelling near a week, and our hunters were so fortunate as now to kill a deer. We encamped at the foot of a hill, so as to be screened by it from the keen northern blasts, and have the benefit of the sun. During our stay at this camp, the old chief killed another deer, which, with raccoons and porcupines, afforded us plenty of food.

The Indians made an offering of the oil, and part of the flesh of the deer, to the *Great Spirit*, by burning it. This I took to be their thank offering for their success in finding a supply of provisions. Before they left the encampment they burned some tobacco; the design of this I did not so well understand. Soon after we began to march, I saw the marks of a cane in the snow, and as the Indians do not use them, I supposed we were overtaking some prisoners. The second day after I saw the cane tracks, we came up with a company of Indians, and here I saw the old Indian who had the cane.

The moment I saw him my attention was arrested by his very grave and ancient appearance. His head was whitened over with, I have no doubt, the frosts of more than one hundred winters, and still he travelled, and kept pace with the horses and young men, from morning till evening. This was the most aged Indian which I saw during my sojourn with them. Their old men are much more vigorous and free from infirmity than ours. They walk erect, and command great respect from all the younger—their counsel is heard with profound attention and respect.

During the month of March the Indians sent to their town for corn. We fared better now, but the corn did not last long; so we were soon thrown back upon what game we could kill in the forests.

From what I could learn, the Indians had adopted me into their family, in the room of a young man who had fallen in battle. Soon after we reached this, the place of our winter quarters, the father-in-law of my Indian dressed me up in Indian costume, made me a bow and arrows, and started me out with his boys to learn to shoot. I was then in the twenty first year of my age. This was our exercise during the cold weather, and afforded me much amusement, as I had none with whom I could converse. We had many a hunt through the woods with our bows and arrows, but I could not learn to use them to much purpose. Sometimes I was permitted to have a gun, and go on a hunting expedition, but was always unsuccessful—I could kill no game. I once saw the Indians proceed to kill a bear which had holed himself up for the winter. The scratches upon the bark was the sign. They then surrounded the tree, and all being ready, they gave a loud yell; the bear appeared, we all fired instantly, and among hands the bear came tumbling down. Soon after this, our old chief killed a very large bear—one of uncommon size even in that country, where they were large and plenty. He brought home a part of it, and on the next day sent out three of his sons, an old man who lived in the family, and myself, to bring in the remainder.

The snow was deep, and we had to travel three or four miles to the place. We took our loads and started to camp. The old Indian mentioned above had on snow shoes in order to walk without sinking; the toe of one of his shoes caught in a small snag which threw him face foremost into the snow, and being heavily laden with bear meat, the strap to which it was suspended came over his arms, and made it very difficult for him to rise. Without thinking where I was, and the danger I was in, I laughed at the old man struggling under the heavy pressure of his bear meat. Fortunately he did not perceive me; one of the young men shook his head at me, giving me to understand that I was risking my life. I discovered that he was also amused, but was afraid to manifest it.

Our hut was now well supplied with meat, the finest that the country could furnish. I flattered myself that we should not want soon again; but to my utter astonishment, our old squaw, my Indian's moth-er-in-law, sat up the whole night and cooked every ounce of it! And worse yet—to my great discouragement, the neighbours were called in next morning, bringing wooden dishes along with them, and after many ceremonies, the whole was divided between the company, who eat what they could and packed off the balance.

There were times when we were very scarce of provisions. On one occasion, I remember, we had for dinner a small piece of bear meat, which, I suppose, had been sent in by some of the neighbours. Our old mother cooked and placed it in a wooden bowl, which was all the china we had. Our dog was looking on with interest, being nearly starved; and when the old lady turned her back, he sprang in upon the meat and started with it in his mouth. The old squaw, with great presence of mind, seized him by the throat to prevent him from swal-lowing it. She succeeded, and replacing it in the bowl, we eat it, and were glad to get it. The Indian women are doomed to a hard life. They do the drudgery. In removing from one camp to another, they pack the goods and children—the men carrying only their guns. I have seen the women wade into the water to their waists in cold freezing weather.

Among the Indians, I saw several persons who had lost the tip of their nose. This was strange, especially among the females. But since, when I was in Detroit, I learned that this was a mode of punishing adultery and fornication among some tribes. I am unable to vouch for the correctness of this statement.

I will here give the reader the history of a corn dance which took place sometime this winter. Our squaws had brought in some corn from the towns. The neighbours were called together, neither to eat, nor drink, but to dance. Considerable preparations were made. Everything was removed from near the large fire that was burning in the centre. The company consisted of grown persons only. One was chosen to make music, which he did by singing and rattling a gourd with shot, or beans in it. They danced round the fire in single file, the men in front.

The women, whilst dancing, keep their feet close together, and perform the exercise by jumping. The men sling their arms most violently and awkwardly, and stamp their feet so as to make the earth sound. They kept up this exercise until a late hour in the night. All seemed to partake of the joy, which they considered to be of a sacred character. It was a thanksgiving for a supply of corn, and the near approach of spring. This dance was finished by a young Indian, selected for the purpose, who performed the closing exercise with great animation. They now all quietly returned to their homes without taking any kind of refreshment.

I soon become satisfied that man in a state of nature laboured under many and serious disadvantages, particularly in the art of preparing their food. Though modern refinement has no doubt carried this matter too far, we may with safety venture to say that man in an uncultivated state falls as far below what is fit and proper for human health and comfort as refinement has gone beyond.

The very best they can do is to make their corn into a kind of small hominy, which they do by the very hardest method, that of pounding it in a mortar—and this labour is performed by the women—after which it is boiled something like half an hour, when it is eaten without salt or anything else with it. But frequently it is prepared without this process, by boiling the corn just as it comes from the ear until a little softened. They seem perfectly satisfied with this alone, once or twice a day without anything else, for they scarcely ever eat meat and corn at the same time. But they eat most enormous quantities, without any apparent rule as to time or quantity. I have known them to eat several times heartily in the course of a few hours; and perhaps the next day hunt all day without eating anything at all. I think it probable that it would hardly have taken all that we saw and experienced to have satisfied even Volney himself, that the civilized is greatly to be preferred to the savage life.

At this camp I also witnessed the mode of cleansing their bodies. They bent hickory poles in the form of wagon bows, and covered them over with blankets. They then took with them a bowl of water and a large hot stone. Two went in together; they poured the water upon the hot rock, and remained within fifteen or twenty minutes, sometimes singing and rattling the old shot gourd. They would then come forth covered with sweat, and sometimes plunge themselves instantly into the river which was at hand.

Perhaps it would be proper here to notice the mode of worship of the Indians. I speak only of the outer form: I know but little of the object of their worship as I did not understand their language. There appears to be some similarity between them and the Jews. Their sacrifices and fasts are frequent. Their fasts are promptly and faithfully attended to. Only one member, however, of the family fasts at a time, which he does for several days together, eating nothing until the afternoon. They treat their females at the birth of their children in a way to remind one of the Jewish custom. See Lev. 12 chap. At such times—let the season be as it may—the woman is compelled to camp out in the woods by herself, and there remain for a certain number of days. And when she is allowed to return to the camp of the family, she must cook in a separate vessel for so many days longer.

Our old man was very fervent in his devotions, especially in his prayers. I never saw anything like idolatry among them.

They are particularly careful to entertain strangers. They are also very hospitable among themselves—they will divide the last morsel with each other. Indians travelling, find homes wherever they find wigwams. If there is only provision enough for one, the stranger gets it, and gets it freely. When any are fortunate in hunting, and it is known to them that others want provisions, they send them a part of theirs without waiting for them to send for it.

You have been presented with the manner in which we spent our time during the cold weather, until sugar-making came on; and now we found work enough. We removed to a beautiful grove of sugar trees, and near the centre of it we pitched our camp, which is the Indian mode. We soon made a quantity of sugar, and some of a fine quality. We used molasses and sugar with our venison and bear meat; and sometimes we made our meals upon sugar and bear's oil, which was better living than the reader might suppose without being acquainted with the dish.

The Indians are sometimes very filthy in their diet. They will kill a deer and take out the entrails, rip them up, turn out the contents, shake them a few times in the snow, throw them for a few moments upon the fire, and devour them like hungry dogs. When they kill a deer with young, the young are considered as a choice dish. They roast them whole. They will eat every animal, and at every part of it, from the bear to the polecat.

Shortly after the breaking of the ice, the old father, one son, and myself, left camp for an otter hunt. We ascended the river, placing traps where we discovered that otters had passed up and down the banks. This we did during the first day, leaving them until our return. We encamped during the first night on the bank of the river. We had nothing to eat. We spent the whole of the second day in hunting, without any success; it was a cold rainy day, and we lay down the second night without a mouthful to eat.

On the morning of the third day the old man left the camp very early, and about twelve o'clock returned, bringing with him two pheasants; they were put into the pot immediately. I feared my portion would be small, as the Indians, when hungry, eat most enormously; but another pheasant was heard near the camp, which the Indian succeeded in killing. It was soon in the pot, and fearing lest the Indians should eat up theirs and then want mine, I did not wait until it was properly cooked before I went to work upon it. We soon devoured the three pheasants without either bread or salt. After this fine dinner we returned to camp again. We examined our traps but found no game.

The spring of the year now came—the ice and snow began fast to disappear—and I now began to think more of home than I had done during the cold season. When the sun began to shine warm, and the birds to sing around me, I would often retire from the camp where I could think of home, and weep, without being discovered. During the time spent in these lonely retreats, which I sought often for the purpose of reflection, Shelbyville, Kentucky, the place of my home, would rise up before my mind with all its inhabitants and endearments. I would think of friends and youthful associates—of the green over which I had played when a boy a school—and of the church to which I gave my hand as a seeker of religion a few months before I left; and of my aged parents, who I knew needed my assistance.

These reflections crowding upon me at once, together with the difficulty and danger of making an escape, would at times almost overwhelm me with sorrow and despair. But the kindness and sympathy manifested toward me by the Indians, and particularly by the wife of the man who took me a prisoner, took off a part of the burthen. This poor heathen woman, who knew nothing of civilization, and the softening influences of the Gospel, nevertheless showed that the tenderness and affection which the Gospel requires were deeply imprinted upon her heart. I had another source of comfort: I found among the Indians a piece of a newspaper printed at Lexington, Kentucky, which I suppose had wrapped up the clothes of some of Captain Hart's men, and thus fell into the hands of the Indians at Raisin. This I read over and over, again and again. I would frequently try to learn the Indians the letters and their sounds; this to them was a very pleasing employment.

The Indians now began to prepare to return to Detroit. This was very encouraging to me, for I now began again to indulge a hope that one day I should yet be free, and reach my friends at home. All hands turned out to making bark canoes. We made two for each large family. In these canoes we ascended the river upon which we had for some time been encamped, until we came to the very head spring—I had no means of ascertaining the name of this river—we then took up our canoes and carried them three or four miles, to the head waters of a river that empties into Lake Erie between the Rivers Raisin and Detroit. The ridge over which we carried our canoes divides the waters of Lake Michigan and Lake Erie.

After entering this stream we advanced finely, finding fish in great abundance. I now began to feel quite cheerful, and things put on a different aspect. This was one of the most beautiful little rivers I ever beheld—I could see the fish at the bottom where the water was ten feet in depth—its beauty was much heightened by passing through several small lakes, the waters of which always enlarged—perhaps increased its waters one half. These lakes were bordered round by various kinds of shrubbery bending over the water. It was now, as near as I could guess, about the first of May, and the scenes were indeed beautiful to one who had been freezing and starving in a northern winter, almost naked—and now turning, as he fondly hoped, his face homeward. I became more and more anxious to escape, as the prospect opened before me.

I had several times formed in my mind plans by which I thought I might escape, but being young and unacquainted with the woods, and knowing that I must be a distance from any of our forts, I was afraid to attempt it; but now, as I believed I was not far from Fort Meigs, I determined to make the attempt. For this purpose I gathered up my bow and arrows, which had laid in the bottom of the canoe for some time, and which I did not intend to use any more, but I wanted them as an excuse to get out and take such a start, without being suspected, as would enable me to make good my escape. We encamped on this river several days; waiting, I suppose, for orders from the British.

During this time I prepared myself for the escape, but unfortunately for my design, the camp was on the wrong side of the river, and I could not take a canoe without being discovered, the camp being immediately on the bank of the stream. In a few days we continued our journey. About this time I saw the first bread since I had been taken prisoner. Some of the Indians had been to the settlement and obtained about half a gallon of flour; they prepared it in their homely way, but I thought it the best bread that I had ever tasted.

On our way down the river, as we came to the road leading from River Raisin to Detroit, we fell in with some Indians who had been at Dudley's defeat. There was a young man with them, a prisoner; the Indians told me by signs to talk with him. When I approached and spoke to him, he seemed astonished, for he had taken me for an Indian; but when he discovered my being an American he was greatly rejoiced. He asked many questions about the Indians, and if I thought that they would sell him. I told him I thought they would not, as I had been their prisoner since the battle at Raisin, and they had not offered to dispose of me. I farther told him I thought his hopes of getting away soon, if ever, gloomy.

He gave me a most horrible account of the defeat of Colonel Dudley, and the slaughter and massacre of his men—and expressed fears that General Harrison would be taken. This was bitter news to me. While we were talking, the Indians stood around and seemed to catch at every word, and watch every expression of our faces—showing the greatest anxiety to know what we said. They would laugh, and look at each other and speak a word or two. It seemed to afford them pleasure to hear us converse. But the time having arrived for us to proceed on our journey, we parted—his company was going by land, and ours by water, to Malden. If I heard the name of the young man I have forgotten it. He was genteel and intelligent. He informed me that he was a surgeon.

I never saw him again, and think it probable that he was killed by the Indians—I am inclined to this opinion because the Indians, we understood, brought in and offered for sale, that spring, all which they did not intend to kill. I think if he had been brought in I should have seen him. Some, it is highly probable, were put to death in the room of those of their friends who had fallen in battle.

We encamped at night, after we saw the young man named above, on an island not far from Malden. The next day we arrived, and the Indians took me down into the town, where I passed for an Indian. It was very unpleasant to me to hear such swearing and profanity— I soon left, and returned to the camp. In a few days we went up the river to the neighbourhood of Detroit, and pitched our tent near the spring wells on the bank of Detroit River. Soon after our arrival arrangements were made with the British Commissary to draw rations of bread, and sometimes fish. They had the number of the family put down in writing, which the Indians were to present before they could draw the supply.

The old Indian, having by some means ascertained that I could write, fell upon a stratagem to increase the quantity of bread. He furnished me with a slip of paper, and proposed that we should alter the number of our family, and make it larger; I did so, and made it about double. I went up with the note myself the first time, to see how it would take. The Indians gave me a horse and bag, and sent a young man of another family with me as a guard, the distance being several miles. The young man obtained his bread sooner than I did, and left me alone. I, after so long a time, got my bread and started; as I passed through the streets of Detroit, a lady spoke to me from an upper window, and said: "Are you not a prisoner, sir?"

"I am, madam."

"Why do you not leave the horse in the street and go to the fort then?"

I told her I was afraid; but did not say I lacked confidence in the British. I feared they would not protect me, but deliver me up if the Indians should demand me.

I went on toward home, and when I got in sight I discovered that they had become uneasy, for the most of them were looking out towards Detroit. When they saw me they raised a great yell, and received me and my bag of bread with great joy.

Some time shortly after this the old man dressed himself up in the finest kind of Indian style, for he was a chief. He greased his face, and then pounded and rubbed charcoal on it until he was as black as a negro. He then painted my face red, and we started together to town, he walking in front. As we passed along the streets the people were very free in making their remarks upon us. "There goes a *mulato*," said one, &c., &c. I seemed to pay but little attention to what was said, but followed my old Indian about from place to place.

In a few days they sent me over to Sandwich, to exchange skins for boiled cider. I succeeded; and they drank it hot, that it might produce the greater effect; their only design seeming to be to produce intoxication. They are liberal with everything they possess but rum. I once saw an Indian give another a dram, and being afraid that he would take too much, he first measured it in his own mouth, and then put it into a tin cup for his friend to drink.

Whilst we were here I saw Indians take medicine. I did not ascertain what kind of medicine it was, only it was something which they gathered from the woods. They boiled it down until it became thick and black. They dug a hole in the ground—furnished themselves with a kettle of warm water and a piece of inner bark—after they took two or three portions of this stuff, they laid down flat upon the ground, with their mouths over this hole, and commenced vomiting. They would then drink large draughts of warm water, thrust the piece of bark down their throats and vomit again. This course they would sometimes pursue for hours together, until one would think that they were almost dead; but they would leave off this vomiting business and go about as though nothing had disturbed them. I heard nothing of any sickness before this medicinal course was commenced, from which I inferred that they took medicine in the spring season whether sick or well.

Not far from our encampment was the grave of an Indian who had been buried several weeks. An old squaw raised an alarm, saying that he had been heard to make a noise. The Indians ran with all haste to the grave—I went too to see what was to be done—but although they listened with their ears upon the ground, and then stamped with their feet, and scratched in the earth, the Indian lay still and dead in his grave.

I learned from the preparations in camp that the squaws were soon to go out to the Indian towns and raise corn, and that I was to go with them. I resolved that I would not go, if my escape should cost me my life. I began immediately to think and plan some method of escape; but every way appeared to be hedged up; there were Indian camps in every direction; there was some faint prospect of success down the river. I also thought of risking myself in the hands of the British, but, as I before said, I could not trust them; and it was well for me that I did not, as I afterwards, to my sore affliction, found them haughty and very inhuman to American prisoners. I wish this censure to rest only upon the British officers, as many of the soldiers would have treated us kindly if it had been in their power.

Just at this crisis, however, an half Indian, who spoke English, came to our camp. I took this opportunity of communicating to the Indians my desire of being sold to the inhabitants of Detroit, who were purchasing prisoners from the Indians, Here I run a great risk—I knew not that they would not instantly kill me for making such a request. No sooner had the half Indian told my wishes, than every eye was fixed upon me; some seemed astonished, and others angry, because I would think of leaving after having been adopted into the family. They soon made signs that I might go, and the old man began to look out for a purchaser. Some of them treated me coolly from that time until I left. A Frenchman came to our camp, and offered a young horse for me—we went several miles down the river to see the horse—the Indian and Frenchman talked a long time—the Frenchman showed several other horses—the Indian did not fancy any of them, and there was no trade. I felt disappointed, being very anxious to be swapped off.

On the next day another Frenchman came to camp riding a snug little pony, with mane and tail roached and trimmed. This horse took the old man's eye, and they soon closed the bargain. The long desired hour had come at last. I felt that I was again free from the hand of the wild savage. I packed up the few tattered rags of clothing which were mine, and prepared to leave; but after all, savages as they were, I was sorry when I bid them a final farewell. The wife of the man who took me prisoner had always been kind—she aided greatly to lessen my sufferings—she had often fed me, and when under the rigors of a northern winter, in the wilderness, had thrown a blanket upon my shivering frame at night; she had restrained the young men from imposing upon me, as they would do by taking my food, and my place at the fire.

After Mr. J. B. Cecott, the man who bought me, and I left the camp, the Indians stood and looked after us as long as they could see us. Mr. Cecott took me to his own house, gave me a suit of clothes, and introduced me to his family. Now I felt that home was much nearer, being again among a civilized people who could speak the English language.

And here let me pause a moment to remark—as I am about to leave the Indians, never I hope to spend another winter with them under the same circumstances—that the few months of captivity with this people, were, taken altogether, the most cheerless and solitary of any part of my life of which I have any recollection. Though many years have rolled by since the events transpired, the impression they made upon my mind is almost as fresh as ever.

Several things contributed to render the scene more gloomy. I lost the day of the month, and also the day of the week; every day seemed alike. No person can have an idea, unless they are placed in the same predicament, how it changes the face of things to lose all those divisions of time that we have been accustomed to observe from our childhood. But this was not all; to render the hours more tedious and solitary, there was not one, of all the families that belonged to our company, that could either speak English, or understand one word of it. And thus, day after day, and week after week, passed over without uttering a solitary word, unless sometimes, when a little distance from camp, I would say a word or two just to hear the sound of my own voice; and it would seem so strange to me, that it would almost startle me.

And, in addition to all this, I was almost eaten up by vermin; sometimes almost starved; and shut out from all civilized society; almost literally buried in the snows of Michigan; and in order to prevent actual starvation, the Indians were compelled to remove from place to place, where it was supposed the hunting would be better. This subjected us to greater inconvenience, and often to great suffering from cold, having to clear away the snow, which was very deep.

But the uncertainty, and the improbability, of being released, being constantly upon me, and there appeared not the least gleam of hope until it was announced, by the preparations I saw making in the spring, to go to Detroit.

I have nothing to say against the Indian character—but many things in favour of it—but much against their manner of life. They are a brave, generous, hospitable, kind, and among themselves, an honest people; and when they intend to save the life of a prisoner they will do it, if it should be at the risk of their own. But after all this is said, no one can form any adequate idea of what a man *must* suffer, who spends a winter with them in the snows of Michigan.

But now, that I was released by the friendly hand of a stranger, Mr. Cecott, whom I shall recollect with feelings of gratitude so long as I can recollect anything—I felt more than I shall ever be able to express. Hope, which had almost perished, now began to revive, and the sight of home and friends once more began to be thought of as a matter not altogether impracticable—and that I should set my foot again upon the happy soil of Kentucky.

But disappointment was at the door. Mr. Cecott informed me in a few days that he would be compelled to give me up to the British as a prisoner of war. I gave him my note for the horse which he gave for me, which I paid him about eighteen months afterwards, when I went out to war again, under General McArthur. I think the horse was valued at thirty six dollars—you see what I was worth in money. A number of prisoners were sold at Detroit from time to time, and many of the citizens showed great liberality and humanity in purchasing them. It should be spoken and recorded to their praise, that some of the citizens spent nearly ever thing which they possessed in buying prisoners who had fallen into savage hands, and in furnishing them with clothing and provision.

When I was delivered to the British as a prisoner of war, I was placed in the guardhouse, where we remained all summer. During our confinement we suffered from hunger, and what provisions we had were not good. We had the floor for a bed, and a log for our pillow, all the time. There were six or eight in the fort that had been purchased before I was—they had were taken prisoners at Dudley's defeat.

This was a long tedious summer to me, for we had no employment whatever, but were compelled to lay about the fort from the end of one month to another. A gentleman in Detroit proposed to the officer in command, to be surety for my appearance, if he would permit me to go into the town and work at my trade, but he refused to let me go upon any terms whatever.

At times, during the summer, the streets of Detroit were filled with Indians; and many of them came to see us. In the month of July, we saw them have a young woman prisoner, whom we supposed they had taken from the frontiers of Ohio. We could never learn what disposition they made of her. A company of the Indians from the northwest encamped for several days near the walls of the fort, immediately previous to their going to war. This gave us an opportunity of ascertaining their mode of preparation for war. Among other things, they eat the flesh of dogs.

During our imprisonment here, we were brought to behold a very shocking sight. We saw, in the hands of the Indians, a number of scalps fastened in hoops made for the purpose and hung out before the fire to dry. They had been but recently taken off: and more horrible yet, the most of them were the scalps of females! We remained for sometime upon the fort battery observing their situation and employment before they saw us. When they beheld us, and knew that we were prisoners, they raised the war-whoop instantly in token of victory. They showed the tomahawk, and pointed to the scalps, to tell that they had murdered the persons with the tomahawk. They held up the scalp of a female and showed signs of savage cruelty and barbarity, which I had never seen exhibited before. These things were done in open day, in the presence of the British officers; and those refined gentlemen, who feel that they occupy a place of elevation and superior rank in society, could look upon these shocking mockeries of humanity with the hard heartedness of the savages themselves.

Many of the British soldiers were kind to us in our imprisonment; they would steal us out by night, when the officers were away carousing, that we might get some recreation and refreshment. The officers were haughty and overbearing, doing nothing for our comfort. The joy that I felt in being released from the Indians, soon died amid my rough fare in the British prison. During the summer we were almost entirely naked; and were only saved from becoming completely so by the generosity of Mr. Hunt of Detroit, who gave us each a suit of summer clothes; which was all the clothing that we got until after we arrived at Quebec, sometime in December.

About the first of August, nearly all the soldiers and Indians disappeared from Detroit. We were at a loss to account for this, but supposed they had gone to make an attack upon some of the forts, or frontier parts of the Northwestern Army. It was not a great while until the secret was out. They came home cursing Major Croghan, (they had made an unsuccessful attack upon Lower Sandusky,) and saying that he loaded his guns with nails, slugs, and with anything and everything that came to hand. The faces of some of them were completely peppered with small shot. They lost a number of their best men in this battle.

It is said that Captain James Hunter, sometimes known by the name of "old Sandusky"—whom Congress since presented with a sword as a token of national respect—suspecting that the British and Indians would undertake to storm the fort, right or wrong, swung up a long heavy log, which, in case of extreme emergency, he intended to use as a *dead fall* by cutting loose the ropes which held it upon the walls of the fort. This Sandusky engagement appears to have been a hot business all around.

The well known battle upon the lake, in which Perry was successful, was fought during our confinement in this fort. We heard the report of the guns plainly, and it produced much excitement among all. Every eye was turned toward Malden, and we eagerly caught every word that came from that direction.

A few days afterward they told us that the British had taken Perry and all his fleet. The soldiers laughed at us, and told us that the Yankees knew nothing about fighting on the water—that they could whip us two to one. We had to bear this as well as we could, until we saw great preparations making every where to remove the arms, ammunition, &c., which were sent up the river. We now suspected that they had misinformed us of the result of the battle. When we asked, they told us one thing and then another, until one of the soldiers privately told us the whole tale—that Perry had actually captured the British fleet—and that the Yankees were coming upon us in great numbers, and were just at hand. We now turned the tables upon them—it was our time to be merry.

Every day increased the hurry and confusion; boats and small vessels were ascending the River Detroit, bearing off arms, provisions, and every species of property, belonging to the British. It was a time of joy to the citizens of Detroit, generally, to see the Indians and British leaving so rapidly: and we were looking almost hourly to behold the Kentuckians appear in sight. We were, however, hurried up the river, as there was no opportunity to escape. The Indians were always kept in the rear during a retreat, and stood between the British and danger. If I had kept the day of the month, I could tell where Harrison, Shelby, and Johnson, were at the time when we left Detroit. Not knowing the position of the American Army, it was fruitless to hazard an effort to escape.

Our British masters crowded us into a vessel which was loaded with arms and ammunition, without provisions or any arrangements for our comfort on the way. As we ascended the lake, we ran aground near the mouth of the River Thames, and were detained two days; during which time we were compelled to unload and reload the vessel. All this time we had nothing to eat but what we could pick up, like dogs, from the offal of the ship. Here I was tempted, and worse yet, yielded to the temptation, to steal something to eat, and risk consequences. The British officer had some beef hung out on the stern of the vessel, I took some of it, and we eat it. The meat was tainted; yet it was sweet to us, not because it was stolen, but because we were starving.

After we had succeeded in getting the vessel over the sandbar, the wind was unfavourable, and the British officer determined to abandon her, and (after getting her up near Dalton's she was burned to prevent the Americans from making any spoils,) here we were put on shore, and walked, hungry and faint, fifteen miles to Dalton's, where we were guarded closely. This was only the beginning of hard times. We discovered the determination of the British to send us down through Canada, and consequently began to lose all hope of seeing the American Army. A guard of British and Indians was prepared to take us on.

A cart load of provision was started with us, but we never saw it after the morning on which we left Dalton's. Why this provision was started, and not suffered to proceed, we never could even guess. The officer was very rigorous, and would not suffer us to stop and procure any refreshment, but drove us onward like cattle going to market. The second night after we left Dalton's, we encamped in the woods. They now kept a close watch over us—and we were as eagerly looking for an opportunity to escape. Had we foreseen the sufferings that were ahead, we should, at least some us, have made the attempt to escape at every hazard.

As stated above, our provisions were left behind, and we were under the dominion of an unfeeling wretch, who would but very seldom even suffer us to go into a house to ask for a morsel of bread. He would march us hard all day, and at night put us into a barn or stable to sleep. We often travelled in the rain, and then laid down without fire in our wet clothes to try and rest. This journey of about five hundred miles by land, and four hundred by water, we travelled, in that cold and rainy country, with our thin gingham clothes, given to us by Mr. Hunt of Detroit: some of us were without shoes and coats; and we lived upon potatoes and turnips just as we could pick them up as we passed by farms.

This part of the journey, from Dalton's to Burlington Heights, was, perhaps, the most painful of any; not being permitted whilst at Detroit to take much exercise, and being forced on almost beyond our strength, rendered it painful beyond expression. And that was not all: the officer of the guard, being a churlish and tyrannical man by nature, failed not to make use of the little brief power committed to him for the occasion, to make our sufferings the more insupportable. It seemed to afford him a pleasure to "add affliction to our bonds." On some occasions, after travelling hard all day in the rain, and having no other lodging but a barn or stable, we had some difficulty in getting fire enough, or getting admittance to it, sufficient to dry our clothes.

On this part of the journey, in addition to suffering from the cold rains, and from being compelled to lie down in our wet clothes, we were almost literally starved. On leaving the vessel on the Thames, I found a canister which had been emptied of the shot; this I took with me, which served to cook our potatoes, turnips, and peas, when we could get them, and when our cruel commander would give us time for it; but to add still more to our inconvenience, one of the Indian guard, on returning from Burlington Heights, stole even that from me. This was done by stratagem, (and, by-the-by, the Indians are not slow at it.)

As some of them had to return from that place, and were preparing for the journey, one of the party come to me and asked the loan of my cooking vessel. I very readily loaned it to him, not suspecting any design; but finding him rather tardy, I made application for it: he gave me to understand that he was not done with it; and being compelled to march immediately, I had to leave it behind. We sometimes had pickled pork, which I generally eat raw. The people in that country raised peas, which they mowed and put away vines and all together for their cattle. We would, when lodging in barns and stables, make beds of these, and shell out and eat the peas, and also take some along with us to eat by the way.

I shall not attempt to notice all the particulars of this painful march, from the Thames to York, and from York to Kingston. It was almost an uninterrupted scene of suffering from the beginning to the end. The officer of the guard seemed unwilling to show any kindness himself, or that anyone else should show us any. The remembrance of these things, though twenty six years have rolled between, produces a kind of horror in my soul even at this hour. Here is the way that a company of ragged, naked, and starved, Kentucky boys were driven through the country to be gazed upon and laughed at by the inhabitants of the villages and towns through which we passed.

When we reached York, we were closely confined in jail until another guard was appointed to take us on to Kingston. This was one of the most filthy prisons that I ever saw. Here they had a difficulty in obtaining a new guard: the one which brought us to this place from the River Thames consisted chiefly of Indians, and as they were not willing to proceed any farther, the officer had to look for some of the most vigilant soldiers to take their place. We found all along that they were not willing to risk us with a guard of British soldiers until we arrived at this point, when they supposed there would be less danger of an escape.

We tarried several days at York, and then took the road to Kingston; and the farther we went the worse the travelling became, the weather colder, and our clothing more ragged, &c.

I must not omit to mention a widow lady who resided between York and Kingston. She took all the prisoners into her house, treated them kindly, supplied all their wants, and in every respect showed a kind and feeling heart. If I ever knew her name, I have forgotten it: I should like to record it here.

When we came to Kingston we were again put in a filthy jail. It was now about the first of November, and we were allowed very little fire, and our clothing so thin, that we had to shiver it out the best way we could. Our spirits remained unsubdued, and we felt cordially to despise that tyranny which heaped suffering upon us. We rejoiced that it was in defence of dear liberty that these afflictions had fallen upon us; and we hoped by some means soon to enjoy our liberty again.

The British troops at this place were in regular drilling. The infantry and artillery were daily employed in firing at targets. My attention was specially drawn to their manner of shooting at a target, made of an empty barrel placed out in the lake. This was done that they might, with the greater certainty, fire upon a vessel as it approached the town. We supposed that they were in expectation of an attack from the Yankee fleet upon Lake Ontario. From Kingston we started to Montreal in open boats; if possible this was yet worse than travelling by land, for we could take no exercise to keep ourselves warm.

The rains that fell upon us now, appeared as cold as during any part of winter in Kentucky, and we were still in our thin clothing. The boat was scarcely large enough to contain the seventeen prisoners, and the guard; and not high enough for us to stand up; so we had to sit down on the bottom of the boat, and endure the cold from morning until night. I think we slept but once in a house between Kingston and Montreal, and that was the upper room of an unfinished court house, where we had a small stove, and where we dried our few rags of clothing. At length we came in sight of Montreal; they landed us above the town that they might march us through the city, to be seen as a rare curiosity. Word had reached the town before us, that a number of Kentucky prisoners were to pass through that day; and it appeared that the whole city had collected into that street to see the great sight. The windows and doors were full of ladies, manifesting great eagerness to see Kentuckians. The reader may perhaps imagine my feelings at this time, for I shall not attempt to describe them.

We were now taken to jail as usual, where we were furnished with a good room, and for the first time since we left Detroit our situation was somewhat comfortable. I think we remained here near two weeks. Our old rags of clothes, which were given us by the British soldiers, proved rather an annoyance to us, as the jail was warm and the vermin began to multiply in great numbers. We had no change of raiment, consequently we had no washing done; thus we spent the time at Montreal.

As before remarked, the vermin became very annoying—and having no possible chance of avoiding them, I fell upon the plan of turning my clothes every morning, so as to keep them travelling.

In order to form an adequate idea of these tormenters of the human family, you must be shut up in a hot, filthy prison, with a number of prisoners clothed in filthy rags, and yourself as bad as any of them, with thousands and millions of these bosom friends crawling over you. If that would not make an impression, I don't know what would.

A right regular built Yankee, who had been but recently taken upon the lines not far from Montreal, was brought into the prison a few days previous to our leaving for Quebec. He was discovered, shortly after his arrival, to pick one of those troublers of our peace from his white shirt, and very deliberately lay him down on a bench, after which, taking a small chip between his finger and thumb, succeeded in dispatching him. This manoeuvre afforded some sport for some of us who had learned, by things we had suffered, not to take it quite so tedious. He was told that he would soon learn to kill them without a chip.

At this place we were told by the British that we were eating Yankee beef—that most of their supplies came from the States. As it is not my business, I will forbear censuring; and will content myself with barely stating facts. These things occur very frequently all along the line between Canada and the United States in time of war; and men who profess great patriotism are sometimes found to be engaged in it. Such patriotism as this would scarcely be found in Kentucky.

We left for Quebec in a steam boat, the first built on the St. Lawrence, and arrived there in about twenty four hours. The jail here was less comfortable than the one at Montreal. We were literally in rags, and remained so for many weeks; we had an agent whose duty it was to see that we were provided for, but if my memory serves me, he did not so much as visit the prison for nearly three weeks, and then we were treated by him like so many slaves.

After so long a time, Gardner, the agent, furnished each of us with a suit of coarse clothing. By this time the weather had become excessively cold, and we were removed to the barracks until a prison could be prepared for us upon Cape Diamond, where we principally spent the time whilst we remained at Quebec.

After we removed to Cape Diamond our number was greatly increased. Only seventeen Kentuckians came down together from Detroit; but there were many others taken at different times and places; some sailors, but mostly they were regular soldiers. These had been confined in other parts of the jail, and now, when collected together, we numbered say ninety, all put into one house together. Here we had a small yard where we could take some exercise; this was a great privilege to men who had been so long in close confinement. We were closely locked up at night, and generally under a strict guard. The windows were strongly grated, and we had only light from one side.

Our provisions were scanty and bad; I suffered more from hunger in Quebec than during any time of my long imprisonment. It was not because they had no provisions, but because they chose to starve us. When we were in Montreal they tauntingly told us that we were eating Yankee beef—giving us to understand that they were furnished with provisions from the United States. This scantiness of supply continued through the winter, and we were under the necessity of enduring our sufferings as we could. We were told that British prisoners in the United States fared worse than we did. Our wood was birch, and it served a double purpose; for we burned the wood, and made tea of the bark—this was all the tea or coffee which we drank in the city of Quebec.

The agent allowed us to draw each a few dollars in money; with this we bought articles from those who visited our prison. We were not very economical with our money; it lasted but a short time.

Some of the prisoners were always forming plans of escape, but could never mature them. At one time we were well nigh an elopement, but one proved a traitor, and informed the British officer of the design. The traitor had been in the regular service, and was taken a prisoner somewhere between Canada and the United States. Some offers were made to him, and he meanly enlisted as a British soldier, and divulged ever thing which he supposed would make our condition more miserable. He told of the contemplated escape, and who were the most active as the leaders. On the next day the keeper of the prison came up, and upon examination finding that the account was true, and ascertaining who had cut the holes, he sent the poor fellows to the dungeon, where they were doomed to remain for two weeks upon half rations. After this penance they were permitted to return to their former place. This broke up all designs of escape, as we were closely watched during the remainder of our stay.

After the fellow above named enlisted, strong efforts were made to induce others to follow his example. In order to this, they sent one of the officers who had command of the guard that brought us from York to Kingston, supposing that because we were acquainted with him, he would therefore have more influence with us. He was, however, the last man that should have been sent; we knew him to be sure, but we knew him to be a hard hearted tyrant, who had starved and drove us nearly to death.

We were displeased at seeing him come into the prison, and no sooner had he made known his errand, than we gave him to understand flatly and plainly that deserters were not to be found among us. We expressed our detestation at the conduct of the one who had turned Tory and traitor, and told him if there was no other way of a release from prison, that we would greatly prefer to lie in the fort until we were starved and perished to death. We moreover gave him to understand that we would not be insulted in that manner, and that he would do well to leave the fort—and some of the boys went so far as to take their tin pans, and beating upon them with their spoons, actually drummed him out of the prison. By this experiment they were fully satisfied that it was a most fruitless business to try to induce us to leave our happy government and join theirs.

It was often reported that we would be sent to Dartmoor prison, in England, and there kept as hostages, until the differences between the two governments should be adjusted. We sometimes thought perhaps it might be so, but we scarcely believed anything which they told us; their object no doubt was to alarm, with the fear of crossing the Atlantic, that they might the more easily persuade us to desert. Although this thing bore a very gloomy aspect, and was often a subject of serious conversation among us, yet we were determined, and strengthened each other in the purpose, not to desert, but to endure the worst, and be true to our country.

About this time we learned that Tecumseh, the great Indian warrior, had fallen in the battle at Moravian town. His family was at this time in Quebec; they, in company with some other Indians, came to see us, and manifested great curiosity in taking a good look at Kentuckians—considered by some the rarest beings upon the earth.

Often numbers of people came to the prison to see us—one man, after looking at us for a length of time, manifested great disappointment, and said, "Why, they look just like other people." It seemed from this that an idea prevailed that we were wild men, or an order of beings that scarcely belonged to this earth.

During the time that we remained here Colonel Lewis and Major Madison visited us. Of the latter, the Vice President of the United States lately said in the Senate, that he was a man:

.... of rare patriotism—the most beloved of all the public men of his State—the best among the best—'the bravest of the brave'—who died with never fading laurels upon his brow.

They were accompanied by one or two British officers. After they had duly examined into our situation, Colonel Lewis encouraged us to bear our privations and sufferings in the spirit of true soldiers—saying "that it belonged to the soil of Kentucky to be firm." While this exhortation of the colonel was received by us with great approbation, it evidently was received with indignation by the British officers. This made no manner of difference with Colonel Lewis, who proceeded to make such remarks, and gave us such advice, as he believed were for our comfort.

I thought that the British were inclined to press their rigid military rules upon Kentuckians with more rigor than upon others. They rarely spoke to us, and when they did it was in a manner so haughty that we only felt the more indignant and hostile toward them. We would not conform to those terms of respect which they exacted from their own soldiers. Our feelings, and callings in life had been so very different from those of British soldiers, that we felt as if we lived in, and breathed, a different air.

Toward the latter part of the winter we were, after much entreaty from Lewis and Madison, permitted to write to our friends. Our letters were carefully read by the officers, and every word rigidly examined. I now wrote to my friends, and this was the first certain information that they received of my having survived the battles and dangers which we had passed through, although I had now been away from home about eighteen months. Notices had been in the public prints, written by Hunt, of Detroit, that prisoners had been carried on towards Quebec—but he had no further knowledge of us, or what would be our fate.

Perhaps it was better that we were not permitted to give a history of our sufferings: it would only have more deeply afflicted our friends, and added nothing to our relief.

I wish here to record, that the news of our unsuccessful attempt to escape reached, by some means, the ears of Colonel Lewis and Major Madison, and they being desirous to obtain the particulars, requested that two of our number might be allowed to visit their quarters, which were not far off. Their request was granted, and William McMillan and myself were selected to visit them. We were conducted by a guard, and very closely watched and listened to. We told them of our attempt and defeat. They gave it as their opinion that we could not make a successful escape during the winter season, and that we ought not to attempt it. They told us of the great difficulty we would meet in travelling through the snow in that country, also in crossing the river St. Lawrence, even if we could, undiscovered, pass the guards. However, in case we should make the attempt, they gave us some directions touching the route that we should take if we succeeded in clearing the sentinels and crossing the river.

While writing this, I am reminded of an attempt made by some prisoners to escape about the time that we came to Quebec. They cut the bars out of the prison windows of the second story of the house, and let themselves down by means of their blankets. They were successful in passing the sentinels, and crossing the river, and prospered all the way until they came near the American lines. Now, thinking that they were out of the reach of danger, they halted to take rest and refreshment, and feeling like birds let out of a cage, they felt that they might safely have a little spree; but just as they were in the midst of their frolic, the British pursuers came suddenly upon them, and took them all by surprise. They were not prepared to defend themselves, and had no opportunity to fly; therefore they had quietly to go back to Quebec, and to prison, where they suffered the deep mortification of a failure, and the renewed weight of British oppression.

Some time before we heard the good news of a general exchange of prisoners, I had a violent attack of bilious fever. I laid several days in the prison before I suffered the old turnkey to know my situation. When it was communicated to him, he sent an old man to bleed me and to give me some physic, which gave me no relief; I was therefore removed about a mile from town, to the hospital, where they bled and physiced me enough. I do not recollect how long I remained at the hospital, but I remember that I was there when it was announced that all prisoners were to be exchanged, and that all who were able to go were to be sent away immediately. This was better to me than all the medicine in Canada. The hope of seeing my country and my home, rushed in upon my mind with refreshing power. I told the doctor that I could not stay any longer in the hospital—that I must start if I died on the way.

At first he opposed my going; seeing my resolution, at length he consented. The idea of being kept behind was like death to me sure enough. For some days before this news reached us I had been slowly recovering, but was yet barely able to walk when I left the hospital to return to the prison, where I found the boys making preparations to leave for the United States. We were to ascend the St. Lawrence in a vessel belonging to the British. It was in the month of May when we left this gloomy prison, where we had spent a miserable winter and spring. The recollection of these times are horrible to my mind until this hour. I am sorry that I ever fell into British hands. It appears that the British officers were perfectly destitute of human feelings, so far as we were concerned.

I have no means of knowing generally their characters, and I surely have no wish to defame them generally; I speak only of those into whose hands I fell, and from whom I received such little kindness.

May had not brought warm weather in that country; heaps of drifted snow were to be seen in the mountains north of Quebec; and the northwestern winds were keen and chilling, especially to me in my feeble state. After we boarded our little vessel, we remained several days, I know not what for, in an uncomfortable situation; with but little fire, and exposed to the incessantly blowing winds. This increased again the disease under which I had been labouring, so that I now had chill and fever every day. I was barely able to walk, and more than one thousand miles from home, without money, clothes, or friends that were able to help; yet my spirit did not quail for a moment,—I hoped somehow to get through.

At length we were put into another vessel, and set sail up the St. Lawrence. Thus we continued until we came to the mouth of the River Sorrell, which connects Lake Champlain with the St. Lawrence. We ascended this river for a considerable distance in the same vessel, when we were placed in open boats and carried across the line. It was said, with what truth I pretend not to say, that some of the British soldiers who guarded us made a good use of this opportunity and deserted, and left a land of oppression for a land of liberty and plenty.

We were set on the shore fourteen miles below Plattsburg, and then left to take care of ourselves, having neither money nor food, and almost naked, and some of us sick. We however, used to trials, went forward to Plattsburg—which I reached with the utmost difficulty, shaking one part of the day, and burning with fever the other. We had all been so long in confinement that we travelled slowly, and this enabled me to keep up until we arrived at a large encampment of the American Army, a short distance above Plattsburg on the lake.

Our situation was communicated to the general, who promised to make provision for us, by giving us written passports, and authorizing us to draw rations on the road wherever we could find any belonging to the United States—which was all that we could expect, or all that we asked, as he had no authority to pay us money. We waited a day or two for the fulfilment of this promise, when we renewed our application, telling him our necessities, how long we had been from home, where we had been taken prisoners, our anxiety to pursue our journey—but all to no effect; we only obtained promises. Having renewed our petitions for a week, we began to despair of success, and thought of seeking help from some other quarter.

We were now satisfied that it was the purpose of the commanding officer to detain us there, place difficulties in our way of going home, that thereby we might be induced to enlist; he supposed that we would not certainly undertake such a journey on foot, without money or passports. This did alarm one or two of the company, who took the bounty and enlisted for five years. The rest of us now resolved to make a start towards old Kentucky; but before we left we made one more unsuccessful effort to obtain the necessary papers from the general. By this time a kind and noble hearted young lieutenant, whose name was Frederick, became interested in our welfare, and wrote us a passport to draw upon any supplies belonging to the government. This answered a good purpose where the keepers were young and ignorant, and did not understand their business; but our order was often protested.

Notwithstanding my fatigue and exposure to the night air, and a chill every day, my strength had much increased, yet I feared the fatigues of the long journey before us; but to my astonishment I had the last chill on the evening before we left the encampment—I never had another.

On a beautiful morning, about the first of June, 1814, we left the American Army near Plattsburg, turning our faces towards home with light hearts and little money. I had but twelve and a half cents, and I believe I was nearly as wealthy as any of the company. And now I feel utterly at a loss to describe my feelings. Until now we did not feel entirely free; though in the American camp, we were under sentinels and military restraint. We had been for so long a time in prison, and suffering, that we seemed to have reached a new world almost. We little thought of the journey that was before us, but talked cheerfully of our situation, as we passed many beautiful farms in high promise, situated upon the sides of the lake. Above all, we felt hearts of sincere gratitude to a kind Providence, who had delivered us out of the hands of wild and ferocious savages, and hard hearted tyrants, and had again brought our feet to stand upon the soil of freedom.

We made our way up the lake on the right bank until we came to the ferry, which we found some difficulty in crossing, because we had no money to pay our passage. We told the keeper the true story of our errand—where we had been, and where we were going: after some hesitancy he took us all over without any pay. We then took the road leading to the head of Lake Champlain; some of the people along this road were kind, but others looked upon us with suspicion.

Our appearance was very shabby indeed—the coarse clothes which we received in Quebec, the winter past, were all in rags and dirt, and having no possible opportunity of getting a new supply, we were compelled to appear before all in our way in this garb. Our rags may have been an advantage to us, as they attracted notice, and curiosity would induce many to ask us questions, and thus we would have an opportunity of telling our history, and so gain something to sustain us upon our journey. This afforded us a good opportunity of ascertaining the dispositions of men. Many were suitably affected with our situation, and offered relief; but other cold blooded animals had no compassion—they lived within and for themselves—and we found some so destitute of all sense of respect as even to insult us.

After travelling together a short distance, we began to find that it would be with difficulty that we could travel through that country without money. We consulted together what way would be the best for us to take, and concluded to separate, as beggars had better go in small companies. When we parted, it was with the understanding that we would try to meet again at Oleann Point, on the Alleghany River. Thus we bid each other farewell, and broke off into companies of four. The company to which I belonged took the road leading from the head of the lake to Utica, in the State of New York. This road was mostly turnpiked, which made the travelling worse for us, as we were nearly barefooted, and our feet soon became sore, so that our stages were short. It would be impossible for me to relate the particulars of this journey through the State of New York; but one thing truth compels me to state, and that is, we suffered more from hunger while passing through this State than in all the rest of the way from Quebec to Kentucky.

We found the people generally either too proud or too stingy to give us food, or to treat us like human beings. In passing through the little towns and villages our appearance would immediately attract attention, and in a few minutes the people would gather around us in great numbers; they would ask us a number of questions, which we would fully answer, though they often suspected us for being deserters. We occasionally found in these companies, persons who were touched by our appearance and story, so they would turn out and raise a few shillings to help us on our journey. The money thus raised we considered as common property, to be used for the benefit of all. We made it last as long as possible, by always purchasing the cheapest articles of food, and never spending any unnecessarily.

When we arrived at Utica we found a recruiting party there; and here I picked up a pair of old shoes which had been thrown away by the soldiers; these enabled me to travel on the turnpike with more ease and speed. We found but few who were willing either to feed or lodge us without pay, though we only asked to lie upon the floor. Some absolutely refused to give us any shelter at all. I will here relate a case, and if I knew the name of the individual I would record it as a warning to anyone who might be tempted to treat any poor sufferer in like manner.

After travelling hard all the day, we called at a house and asked the man the favour to stay and lie upon the floor until morning, at the same time informing him that we had been prisoners for some time, and that we were on our way to Kentucky, our native State, and that we would not ask him for anything else. He told us pointedly that we could not sleep in his house. We then asked to sleep in the shop, (he was a wagon maker:) this he also refused; we then told him that we were much fatigued, and would be glad to have permission to lie down in his barn. He then refused in the most positive manner; telling us that there was a tavern about a mile ahead, and as they had the profit of travellers, they should have the trouble also. We left him to his conscience, and walked on toward the tavern, feeling that we were strangers indeed in a strange land, driven from door to door, fatigued and hungry, without one cent in our pockets, knowing not where we should find shelter; and returning too from fighting the battles of the country we were now passing through so poorly requited.

At length we came to the tavern, and by stating our misfortunes we succeeded in gaining permission to sleep on the floor. Soon after our arrival supper was announced, but nothing was said to us. We laid down on the floor of the bar room hungry, tired and sleepy. If we had received such treatment in an enemy's country, we would not have been surprised, but we had been out fighting for the liberties of this very people—this made our sufferings the more acute. We made an early start next morning, supposing that the chance for breakfast would be as gloomy as that of the supper had been. We determined to go forward as far as possible, hoping soon to find another kind of people, who would help us.

When we applied in the evening for permission to lie in the barn, and were refused, there was a gentleman present who overtook us a day or two afterwards, and reminded us of the treatment, and that he was present; he gave each of us some money—he said that he had no money when he first saw us.

Not far from this hard place, we met a man of quite a different feeling. Near sunset we were passing his house, when he called to us and asked if we had any money; we told him we had none: "Well, you had better stop here with me and stay all night, for the man who keeps the next house is a Tory, and will not permit you to stay without money." I need hardly say that we acceded to his proposition. We were treated with kindness and hospitality, and for once fared well. This was a set-off to some former cases.

After we had passed through the thickly settled parts of New York, we came to the Genesee country, which was at that time but thinly inhabited. We were now told that we would find serious difficulties in passing on without money; on the day that we entered what was called the wilderness we were entirely destitute, and had very serious fears of suffering more than we had yet been called to endure; but as our fears were rising to the highest pitch, we unexpectedly met a young officer belonging to the United States service; he inquired into our history carefully, and becoming satisfied with the account which we gave him of our capture and sufferings, he kindly gave us one dollar a piece, which was sufficient, with rigid economy, to carry us through the most dreaded part of the wilderness.

It may appear to the reader that I have given, a very cheerless and rigid account of the people along the road that we travelled through the State of New York; I am certain of the truth of the history, for a man starving knows when he receives anything to eat, and also when he is refused. I am as certain of this part of the history, as that I was in the battle, and wounded at the River Raisin. Whether we fell upon the only niggardly people that lived in that part of the country, or whether the people were mostly Tories there, I have no means of determining.

It may be asked why I record these things? It may seem harsh to speak of them; it was much harsher to feel them. If people will sin publicly, and drive starving begging soldiers from their doors with contempt, those soldiers, if they should live to reach home, and should write an account of their trip, will be very likely to refer to such treatment. If those folks are yet living, a sermon upon "be careful to entertain *strangers*," might not be entirely without its good effects upon them.

After passing through this wilderness, we began to draw near to Oleann Point, the place where we had agreed to meet again when we parted at the head of Lake Champlain. One company overtook us on the same day that we arrived at Oleann. Here we had intended to take water, but we could hear of no craft going down the river. Our money was gone, and provisions were scarce and dear, so we could not stay long here. Necessity, the mother of invention, drove us to seek out some way of getting on.

We numbered eight persons at this time; I remember the names of Philip Burns, Patrick Ewing, Simon Kenton, Thomas Bronaugh, William McMillan and Thomas Whittington. At length we concluded to build a raft of slabs that we found lodged against a bridge; so we all went to work; having walked so far, our wind was pretty good, and got our raft completed by sunset—on Sunday too. We then procured some bread, and set sail down the river a little before dark, not knowing what was before us, whether there were dangerous passes, or falls in the river—such was our destitute situation, that we were compelled to go on. Our provisions were nearly out, and Indians chiefly inhabited the country along the river down towards Pittsburg.

During the night we had some difficulty in passing the drift at the short bends that are in the Alleghany, but went on tolerably well until next morning about breakfast time. I had laid myself down upon the dry part of the raft and fallen asleep, not having slept any during the night, as there was not room for more than two or three to lie down at once. We now came in contact with a driftwood, and the current was so strong that the raft was taken under almost instantly—we scrambled up on the drift, and after some difficulty got ashore. The raft came out below, and went on; and then we were left on foot again, among the Indians called Corn Planters.

Fortunately for us, we had taken a Yankee passenger aboard our raft, who had some money with him, with which we bought a canoe from an Indian in which we came down the river until we reached Pittsburg. Before we reached Pittsburg we met a recruiting party at the mouth of French Creek; the officer was very kind—he furnished us with a room to sleep in—gave us flour and whiskey. His object was to enlist some of us; we did not tell him that we would not enlist; we sat up however and baked bread enough whilst the others were asleep to last us to Pittsburg; and before the officer was out of his bed in the morning, we were paddling on towards home.

When we arrived at Pittsburg, we sold the canoe for five dollars, and purchased bread, and almost immediately took passage on a salt boat bound for Kanawha. But whilst we were in Pittsburg we there saw the British soldiers that guarded us at Detroit prison—they had been taken at the Battle of the Thames—they were at liberty to go to any part of the town, and to work for themselves. We took this opportunity to remind them of the difference between their treatment of us, and our treatment toward them; they were compelled to acknowledge the truth, and praised our officers very highly.

We paid our passage upon the salt boat, by working at the oars, all except myself, who was the cook for the company. When we floated down as far as Kanawha we were there set upon the shore, and were once more compelled to look about for the means of continuing our journey. After we had been there a few hours we saw a raft of pine plank floating down the river; we hailed the owner, asked for a passage, and were taken aboard. On this raft I floated down to Maysville, where, thanks to a superintending Providence, I once again set my feet upon Kentucky soil, and breathed the air of my native State.

Now I was almost naked; no person, as well as I can remember, had offered me a single article of clothing since I left Quebec. I had exchanged my pantaloons, given to me in prison, for an old pair which I found on the boat, thrown away as useless by some of the boatmen; my shirt had, by slow degrees, entirely disappeared; I had some where picked up an old coat that had been the property of some regular soldier—these two articles constituted my wardrobe, entire—I was barefooted, but had an old hat.

My companions had all left me higher up the river, and gone across the country as a nearer way home. When I left the raft and went into the town my situation excited attention, and soon all my wants were supplied. Some gave the stuff, and a number of tailors joined, and in a few hours I was clothed, and furnished with money to bear my expenses home. I felt the difference here between warm and cold hearted people. My anxiety was great to pursue my journey, so I ascended the steep hill that hangs around Maysville, and made my way through Georgetown and Frankfort, to Shelbyville, at which place I arrived on the 20th day of June, *A. D.* 1814.

Here, at length, after an absence of nearly two years, during all of which time I had been exposed to sufferings, dangers and privations, not having slept upon a bed until my return to my native land, I found myself among the friends of my childhood and my own beloved kindred. I had left them, when a mere lad, as a volunteer soldier in the company commanded by Captain Simpson, and I came back to them a man in years, though feeble in strength and frail in appearance. The meeting indeed was unexpected to them, and none can tell the fullness of joy that reigned in my own heart.

A kind and merciful Providence had preserved and sustained me through all the perils with which I was surrounded, and unto Him do I give the praise for my safety. Many years have passed since the occurrences detailed in this narrative took place. I may now almost be classed in the number of old men. My avocations have been those of peace. I have, for nearly twenty years, as an ordained Minister of the Methodist Episcopal Church, endeavoured to teach the mild doctrines of my blessed master. Yet it may not be without its use to my young countrymen to know what their fathers have suffered. I have told them a plain unvarnished tale, which while it may encourage them to be bold in their country's cause, may also, acquaint them with what they owe to the generation that has just preceded them.

W. Atherton.

Note.—On page 22 of the foregoing narrative, mention is made of the reception, by the suffering volunteers, of a seasonable supply of clothes that had been made up and sent to the army by the patriotic ladies of Kentucky. I have, since the commencement of this publication, met with an article that appeared in the Frankfort Commonwealth (when that paper was under the editorial direction of Orlando Brown, Esq.) entitled *Kentucky Mothers,* in which allusion is made to the same transaction. I have thought it not irrelevant to append it to this, as it shows, in a striking manner, the deep devotion to country felt by the ladies of Kentucky, and the extent of the sacrifices they were prepared to make. Although Mr. Brown did not give the name of this noble mother, I have his permission to state that the lady alluded to is the venerable Mrs. Elizabeth Love, who yet, (as at time of original publication), resides in Frankfort, beloved by all for her eminent worth, and characterized by high intellectual endowments associated with fervent piety, unaffected charity, and every trait that dignifies and adorns the female sex.

Kentucky Mothers

The deep interest which passing events are giving to the history of the campaigns of the North-Western Army, naturally sets the memory to work in recalling the incidents that gave them their peculiar character. The achievements of the volunteers under the gallant Harrison, are written in the brightest pages of the records of their country, and must live so long as the human heart thrills at the contemplation of deeds of lofty heroism. But Kentucky does not point solely to her brave soldiers, and challenge admiration for them. Far, far from it; for to the noble mothers and daughters of our State belongs a chaplet of unfading laurels. *They* espoused the cause of their country with an ardour never surpassed in any land under the sun.

Company after company, battalion after battalion, left the State for the scene of war, and although the bloodiest battles were fought, and men came home with thinned ranks and wearied frames, and the wail of the widow and the orphan was loud in the lament for the slain, the fire of patriotism burnt the brighter, and the women of Kentucky, never faltering, still urged on the men to battle. Although we were at that time but a very small boy, well do we remember all that passed under our observation at that stirring period. We remember the letters that were received from the volunteers describing their sufferings from cold and hunger and nakedness, and we remember, too, how the ladies united together for the purpose of sending clothing to the suffering soldiery.

They formed themselves into sewing societies, made hunting shirts, knit socks, purchased blankets and fitted up all kinds of garments that could add to the comfort of the troops. The ladies of the town of Frankfort, alone, sent two wagon loads of clothing to the frontier, which arrived most timely, and warmed alike the hearts and bodies of the volunteers, for they reminded them that such wives and mothers and sisters deserved to be defended at every possible hazard.

A Spartan mother is said, on presenting a shield to her son, to have told him "to return, *with it or upon it.*" It is recorded of another, that when her son complained of the shortness of his sword, she bade him "take one step nearer his enemy and he would find it long enough." And for such sayings as these, the Spartan women have ever since been renowned in history. We remember an incident that occurred in our own presence during the last war, that proves that a Kentucky mother was fully equal in courage and love of country to any of those whose fame has survived for so many ages. We beg leave to relate it, and will do so in as few words as possible.

Soon after the Battle of the River Raisin, where the captain of the Frankfort company (Pascal Hickman,) had been barbarously massacred in the officers' house after the surrender, Lieutenant Peter Dudley returned to Frankfort for the purpose of raising another company. The preceding and recent events of the campaigns had demonstrated to all that war was, in reality, a trade of blood, and the badges of mourning, worn by male and female, evidenced that *here* its most dire calamity had been felt. He who would *volunteer* now, knew that he embarked in a hazardous enterprise.

On the occasion alluded to, there was a public gathering of the people. The young lieutenant, with a drummer and fifer, commenced his march through the crowd, proclaiming his purpose of raising another company, and requesting all who were willing to go with him, to fall in the ranks. In a few moments he was at the head of a respectable number of young men; and, as he marched around, others were continually dropping in. There was, in the crowd of spectators, a lad of fifteen years of age; a pale stripling of a boy, the son of a widow, whose dwelling was hard by the parade ground. He had looked on with a burning heart, and filled with the passion of patriotism, until he could refrain no longer, and, as the volunteers passed again, he leaped into the ranks with the resolve to be a soldier.

"You are a brave boy," exclaimed the captain, "and I will take care of you;" and a feeling of admiration ran through the crowd.

In a little time, the news was borne to the widow, that her son was marching with the volunteers. It struck a chill into her heart, for he was her oldest son. In a few moments she came in breathless haste, and with streaming eyes, to the father of the editor of this paper, who was her nearest neighbour, and long tried friend.

"Mr. Brown, James has joined the volunteers! the foolish boy does not know what he is about. I want you to make haste and get him out of the ranks. He is too young—he is weak and sickly. Mr. Brown, he will die on the march. If he does not die on the march he will be killed by the enemy, for he is too small to take care of himself. If he escapes the enemy he will die of the fever. Oh, my friend, go and take him away."

After a few moments, she commenced again—"I do not know what has got into the boy—I cannot conceive why he wants to go to the army—he could do nothing, he is able to do nothing."

Again she paused; and at last rising from her seat, with her eyes flashing fire, she exclaimed—"*But I would despise him, if he did not want to go!*" That noble thought changed the current of her reflections, and of her grief—she went home, prepared with her own hands the plain uniform of that day for her son, and sent him forth with a mother's blessing. The lad went on with the troops, bore all the toils of the march, was in the battle at Fort Meigs, and fought as bravely and efficiently as the boldest man in the company. The widow's son again came home in safety. Her patriotism has not been unrewarded. Only yesterday I saw that son bending over the sick bed of the aged mother. He is the only surviving child of a numerous family, and has been spared as the stay and prop of her declining years, (as at time of first publication).

Is it any wonder that the Kentuckians are brave and chivalric? Were they otherwise, they would be recreant to the land of their birth, and a reproach to their mothers' milk.

A Journal

Contents

Preface   87

Journal of the Campaign, &c. &c.   89

Narrative of Mr. Timothy Mallary   130

Narrative of Mr. John Davenport   135

The Battle of Raisin   139

Preface

The author of this journal wrote it for his own satisfaction When he returned home he was induced to show it to a number of his acquaintances for their information. Several, on whose judgment he could rely, requested him to publish it to the world. He begs leave simply to remark that he was an eye and ear witness to many things he has narrated. He has represented things as he understood and remembered them. Other facts he obtained from testimony in which he could fully confide. It is worthy of remark that witnesses of probity, in giving their testimony in courts respecting the same things, often differ from one another as to many circumstances, owing to their different capacities, positions, and the like.

It may be expected therefore, that some who were in the army may not exactly agree with the author in all things stated in this journal. Let that be as it may, he is conscious that he sought the most correct information, and that he endeavoured to communicate it in a plain, perspicuous style. If he has made any important mistakes, should those interested convince him of them, in a friendly way, he will use the best means in his power to correct them.

As to the narratives subjoined to this journal, they are short, and he thinks interesting. He is acquainted with Mr. Davenport, and believes him to be a man of veracity. He had no acquaintance with Mr. Mallary before he applied to him for his narrative. His acquaintances will best know what credit ought to be given to him.

The gentlemen who gave the narratives, it is obvious, are the *only persons responsible for the truth of them.*

The whole is with diffidence submitted to the candour of a generous public, by

Elias Darnell.

Journal of the Campaign, &c. &c.

For a few years past differences existed between the United States of America and the Kingdom of Great Britain. Every possible means had been used on the part of the executive and legislative departments of the general government of the United States, to adjust those differences upon honourable and equitable terms. But Great Britain treated every reasonable proposition with haughtiness and contempt, and still persisted in violating the just rights of the Americans, by committing depredations on the high seas and by impressing the citizens of the United States into the service of His Majesty, and employing the savages to murder the defenceless inhabitants of the frontiers. The United States having long borne these outrages with great patience, at length wearied with insults, resorted to the last and most painful alternative of declaring war (which was done on the 18th of June, 1812); and the government having called for volunteers, more than the quota of this State rallied round their country's standard, ready to assist in a vigorous prosecution of the war in order to hasten a speedy and honourable peace.

General Hull having been appointed by the general government to take possession of part of Upper Canada, his forces, amounting to about 3,000, not being considered sufficient to exe cute that design, three regiments of volunteer infantry and one regiment of United States infantry, amounting in all to about 2,300, were called and destined to his assistance.

Agreeably to a general order, the following regiments rendezvoused at Georgetown, August 15, 1812, to wit:—

The first regiment was commanded by Colonel John M. Scott, the fifth regiment was commanded by Colonel William Lewis, the first rifle regiment by Colonel John Allen, the 17th United States regiment by Colonel Samuel Wells; the whole under the command of

Brigadier-General Payne.

16th. The troops paraded early in the morning, and were received by Governor Scott. We paraded again at 10 o'clock , and marched to a convenient place in close order, where the Rev. Mr. Blythe preached a short sermon, and the Honourable Henry Clay delivered an appropriate discourse.

17th. The troops were inspected by Major Garrard.

18th. We drew two months pay in advance. There being a general complaint amongst the volunteers respecting sixteen dollars, which were expected to be drawn in lieu of clothing, Major Graves paraded his battalion and gave them their choice to go on without the sixteen dollars, or return home. Six chose to return; these, to fix an odium upon them, were drummed out of camp and through town.

19th. We commenced our march in high spirits to join General Hull at Detroit, or in Canada. Each regiment, for convenience and speed, marched separately to Newport. We arrived at Newport the 24th; it is 80 miles from Georgetown. It rained most of the time, which made it disagreeable travelling and encamping. These hardships tended a little to quench the excessive patriotic flame that had blazed so conspicuously at the different musters and barbecues.

Here we received information of General Hull having surrendered Detroit and Michigan Territory to General Brock, on the 15th of this instant, while in possession of the necessary means to have held that post against the forces of Upper Canada.[1] This we could not believe until confirmed by handbills and good authority; when thus confirmed, it appeared to make serious impressions on the minds of officers and privates. Those high expectations of participating with General Hull in the laurels to be acquired by the conquest of Malden and Upper Canada, were entirely abandoned.

---

1. To prove that this surrender was not in consequence of the want of ammunition and provisions, it is sufficient to state, upon the authority of official information, that there were thirty-three pieces of cannon, twenty-five of which were brass, and eight iron, which were well manned and supplied with ammunition. For the muskets, seventy-five thousand cartridges were made up, besides besides twenty-four rounds in the cartouche-box of each man. In the magazine were sixty barrels of powder, and one hundred and fifty tons of lead. In the contractor's store were at least twenty-five days provisions; and in the adjacent country considerable supplies could have been had, besides three hundred head of cattle, under an escort commanded by Captain Brush, at the River Raisin.   An Ohio Volunteer.

We drew our arms and accoutrements, and crossed the Ohio on the 27th. Our destiny was thought to be Fort Wayne.

The following general order will show some of the evolutions which were performed by this army while on its march:

Headquarters, Cincinnati, August 23, 1812.

The troops will commence their march in the direction to Dayton, by Lebanon, at an early hour tomorrow morning. The *generale* will be beat instead of the *reveillé*, the tents will then be struck, the baggage loaded, and the line of march taken up as soon as possible.

The commandants of the several corps will immediately commence drilling their men to the performance of the evolutions contemplated by the commander-in-chief, for the order of march and battle. The principal feature in all these evolutions is that of a battalion changing its direction by swinging on its centre.

This, however, is not to be done by wheeling, which by a large body in the woods, is impracticable. It is to be formed thus: the battalion being on its march in a single rank, and its centre being ascertained, the front division comes to the right about, excepting the man in the rear of that division, who steps two paces to the right; at the same time the front man of the second division takes a position about four feet to the left of the man in the rear of the front division, and dresses with him in a line at right angles to the line of march. These two men acting as marks or guides for the formation of the new alignment at the word—"Form the new alignment, March!" the men of the front division file round their guide, and form in succession on his right. At the same time the men of the rear division file up in succession to the left of the guide, and dress in a line with him and the guide of the front division. This manoeuvre may be performed by any number of men, by company and platoon as well as battalion.

Wm. H. Harrison,
Major-General Commanding.

31st. General Harrison overtook the army between Lebanon and Dayton. He was received joyfully by all the troops as commander-in-chief, with three cheers.

September 1. The army arrived at Dayton, fifty miles from Cincinnati, and was saluted by the firing of cannon. One of the men who were firing the cannon got one of his hands shot off, and the other badly wounded. We arrived at Piqua, September 3, thirty miles from Dayton, on the Big Miami.

4th. Received information of the critical situation of Fort Wayne. Colonel Allen's[2] regiment and two companies from Colonel Lewis's drew twenty-four rounds of ammunition, and started with all possible speed to the relief of that fort.

5th. General Harrison having paraded the remaining part of the army in a circle in close order, delivered a speech to them, stating that he had just received intelligence from Fort Wayne; that it was in great danger of being taken by the Indians and British; he said that we were under the necessity of making a forced march to their relief. He read some of the articles of war, and stated the absolute necessity of such regulations and restrictions in an army, and if there were any who could not feel willing to submit to those articles and go on with him they might then return home. One man belonging to Colonel Scott's regiment made a choice of returning home rather than submit to those terms. Some of his acquaintances got a permit to escort him part of the way home. Two of them got him upon a rail and carried him to the river; a crowd followed after; they ducked him several times in the water, and washed away all his patriotism.

6th. We marched at 12 o'clock —we left all our sick and part of our clothing and baggage at Piqua, in order to make as much speed as possible. On the morning of the 8th, three miles from St. Mary's, one of Captain M'Gowen's company was accidentally shot through the body by one of the sentinels; the surgeon thought it mortal.[3] We marched four miles and encamped near the River St. Mary's, one mile from the fort. General Harrison called the army together and stated, through emergency, we must be on half rations of flour for a few days, but should draw a ration and a half of beef, as he wished to go as light and as quick as possible. He said, "Any who do not feel willing to go on these terms may remain at the fort and have plenty." I know of none that stayed. St. Mary's blockhouse is thirty miles from Piqua, on the River St. Mary's.

9th. We marched through some first-rate woodland, and through

---

2. Colonel Allen stopped at St. Mary's for the remaining part of the army.

3. He died in a few days.

a large prairie of the best quality. It is badly watered; the water in the wagon-ruts was the only drink we could get to cool our scorching thirst, and but very little of that. We encamped near the River St. Mary's, eighteen miles from the fort. At eleven o'clock and at three we were alarmed by the sentinels firing several guns; we formed in order of battle, and stood so fifteen minutes.

The following extract of a general order is designed to show the order of battle for night and day attack:

Headquarters,
Second Crossing of St. Mary's, Sept. 10, 1812.

The signal for a general charge will be beating the long-roll. Officers and men will be upon their arms and in their clothes. Two or more guns firing in succession will constitute an alarm, at which the whole army will parade in the order of encampment (that is, in a hollow square), unless otherwise directed. When a sentinel discharges his gun in the night the officer of the guard to whom he belongs will immediately ascertain the cause, and should he have sufficient reason to believe, on an examination, that an enemy is near, he will cause two guns to be fired in quick succession. Should the firing of a sentinel appear to have proceeded from a cause not sufficient to give an alarm, the officer of the guard will immediately call out all is well, which will be repeated through the army. The same thing will take place upon an accidental fire made in the day.

The order of battle for rear attack will be so far attended with regard to the rear line; the rear battalions of Colonel Lewis's regiment and Colonel Allen's only are to turn upon their centre, while the heads of the front battalions are to close up the front lines, then, facing from the centre, march out until they respectively gain the flanks of the front line. Should the attack be in front, the senior officer nearest the flank battalion will judge of the propriety of bringing up that battalion to form on the flank of the front line. The second battalion of Colonel Lewis's and Colonel Allen's regiments will, in all cases, close up as the leading battalions shall advance, and make room for them. Captain Garrard's troop, forming the rear guard, will also close up and act as circum stances may require.

Wm. H. Harrison,
Major-General Commanding,

10th. The order of march for the infantry was as follows: the first and fifth regiments formed one line in single file on the left, two hundred yards from the road, the 17th United States and the rifle regiments on the right in the same manner: the baggage in the road. The order of march for the horse troops: One of Colonel Adams's battalions of Ohio volunteers was placed at the distance of half a mile in front of the columns of infantry, and marched in columns of companies in files, and in such open order as to cover the whole front of the army. The other battalion of Ohio volunteers formed the right flank guard of the army, at the distance of three hundred yards from the column of infantry, and parallel to it. The Kentucky mounted riflemen on the left, the same distance from the left column of infantry for the left flank guard; Captain Garrard's troop formed the rear guard. We marched twelve miles.

11th. The spies wounded an Indian and got his gun and blanket; our day's march was eleven miles; we stopped earlier than usual in order to make breastworks, and because it was a convenient place for water. We fortified this place very strongly with timber. At 11 o'clock the camp was alarmed by the firing of many guns by the sentinels. The whole army was formed in quick time, the horse troops being in the centre ready to assist any line or to obey any order which might be given. One half of the men were dismissed and retired to their tents for one hour, then they relieved the first half. At 3 o'clock another alarm took place from the sentinels, a general parade was again made. We stood in order of battle for some time. The watchword was "*fight on*" after which this place was called "Fort Fight On."

12th. We continued our march towards Fort Wayne with as much caution as the nature of our hurrying would admit; we expected to meet with the enemy before we reached the fort. In a certain well-known swamp through which we had to pass, we thought probably the enemy would harbour. We passed the swamp unmolested for a mile, we were then alarmed. The rear battalions formed in order of battle but saw no enemy to fight; we immediately resumed our march. This alarm and the one the night pre ceding seemed to shake the boasted valour of some of our bravest heroes.

This day's march was twenty miles to Fort Wayne, through a great deal of first-rate land, rich, level, and well timbered, but badly watered near the road; we suffered extremely for water these three days. Our arrival at this fort gave great joy to the inhabitants, who were one company of regular troops and a few families. The Indians had closely invested the fort for several days, and burned the United States factory and all the other valuable houses which were not inside of the stockading. Three of our men who were caught out of the fort were killed by the Indians. The Indians encamped about the fort two weeks before they made the attack on it, and were admitted in by Captain Ray, the commanding officer of the garrison, who would have surrendered to the savages, had it not been for his lieutenant, who defended the fort with great bravery. Three Indians were killed and a few wounded. Captain Ray was arrested and would have been broken had he not resigned. The fort was well provided for a siege, having in it one hundred men, plenty of provisions, ammunition, four small pieces of cannon and a good well of water.

Fort Wayne is one of the most elegant situations I ever saw, and must be an important place to the United States. Three weeks ago the neighbourhood around the fort would have exhibited a pleasing prospect to those who had seen nothing for several days but a dreary wilderness of one hundred miles. A number of well-cultivated farms with neat houses, in view of the fort, would have excited emotions of pleasure. I suppose there were four hundred acres of land in cultivation. All the houses were reduced to ashes, together with a large quantity of small grain and hay, by the savages; they were principally Pottowatomies; they also destroyed all the stock of every kind about these farms, which was very considerable. Fort Wayne is situated on the south side of the River Maumee, opposite the junction of the River St. Mary's and St. Joseph, which are considerable navigable streams in lat. 41° 40' N. long. 11° 5' west from the meridian of Philadelphia.

We were alarmed by the report of some guns which were fired by the sentinels; we formed in order of battle for half an hour, during which time it rained very hard, and rendered many of our guns unfit to do execution, except the bayonets. The alarm must have proceeded from the timidity of the sentinels.

14th. The whole force was divided and placed under the command of General Payne and Colonel Wells. General Payne's command was composed of Colonel Lewis's regiment, Colonel Allen's and Captain Garrard's troop. Colonel Wells's command was composed of Colonel Scott's regiment, the regulars and the mounted riflemen. General Payne was instructed to destroy the Miami towns at the forks of the Wabash. Colonel Wells was directed against the Pottowatomies village of Elkheart. General Harrison thought proper to go with General Payne; so we proceeded on to the waters of the Wabash; five miles from Fort Wayne we encamped. Next morning we came to an Indian hut and a small cornfield, two miles from our encampment; here all the wagons and baggage were left, and Captain Langhorne's company as a guard; from this place we marched twenty-three miles to an Indian town at the forks of the Wabash; we found the town evacuated; we pulled down some of their houses and built up fires and encamped; we had plenty of roasting ears of the best kind. It is a small kind of corn, shallow grain, and very suitable for roasting ears, which answered us a very good purpose, as we had only a little provision with us.

16th. We marched through their towns, four in number, in the bounds of three or four miles, in which there were fresh signs of Indians. We cut up their corn and put it in piles, sixty or eighty acres, so that it might rot. A variety of beans were found growing with their corn; potatoes, pumpkins, water-melons, and cucumbers were also cultivated by them. Their houses were all burnt by the orders of General Harrison; some of them were built of bark and some of logs. The tomb of a chief was discovered; it was built on the ground with timber and clay, so that no rain or air could enter; the chief was laid on his blanket, his head towards sunrise, his rifle by his side, his tin pan on his breast, with a spoon in it; he was ornamented in their style, with ear-rings, brooches, &c. This is one of the most beautiful places in the western country; the land is level, well timbered, well watered, and the soil equal to any part of Kentucky. Near the town, where the timber has been cut, it is covered with an elegant coat of blue grass.

17th. We got back to the baggage, and found all was well. Captain Langhorne had fortified against the enemy with rails, so that he would have been able to have held his place against a considerable force. We took some refreshments and pursued our journey, and encamped near our former encampment.

18th. We arrived at Fort Wayne, and met with a reinforcement of five hundred mounted riflemen and cavalry, from Kentucky. A man was accidentally shot through the head by one of the mounted riflemen. Colonel Wells's division returned this evening from their route, which was fifty miles from Fort Wayne, on the waters of St. Joseph's River, very much fatigued. They found nothing but deserted houses and corn to destroy, which was about the same amount as was found at the Wabash. Captain Morris's first sergeant (David Irwin) died on the road. One of the light-horsemen wounded a man as he was feeding his horse, believing him to be an Indian.

19th. We encamped in the forks of the river half a mile from the fort. General Harrison not being legally authorized by the general government, as commander of this army, the command, of course, devolved on Winchester. This resignation of General Harrison's was done with much reluctance, as he had placed great confidence in the Kentuckians, and found he was their choice, in preference to General Winchester. The conduct of General Harrison at Tippecanoe, and his familiarity with the troops while on their march to this place, had gained to him a peculiar attachment. General Winchester being a stranger, and having the appearance of a supercilious officer, he was generally disliked. His assuming the command almost occasioned a mutiny in camp; this was prevented by the solicitations of some of the officers to go on.

20th. The Kentucky mounted riflemen started to St. Mary's under the command of General Harrison, in order to pursue the Indians in some other quarter; their number was about fifteen hundred.

21st. We received marching orders to march tomorrow morning at 7 o'clock.

The following general order will show General Winchester's order of march:—

General Orders. Fort Wayne Sept. 22, 1812.
The army will march in the following order, to wit: the guard in front in three lines, two deep in the road, and in Indian file on the flanks, at the distance of fifty to one hundred yards from the centre line, when not prevented by obstructions.

A fatigue party, to consist of one captain, one ensign, two sergeants, two corporals, and fifty privates, will follow the front guard for the purpose of opening the road. The remainder of the infantry to march on the flanks in the following order; Colonel Wells's and Allen's regiments on the right, and Scott's and Lewis's on the left.

The general and brigade baggage, commissaries and quarter masters stores immediately in the rear of the fatigue party. The cavalry in the following order: Captain Garrard and twenty of his men to precede the guard in front, and equally divide at the head of each line. A lieutenant and eighteen men in rear of the whole army and baggage. The balance of the cavalry equally divided on the flanks of the flank lines.

The regimental baggage wagons fall in according to the rank of the commanding officers of the respective regiments. The officers commanding corps, previous to their marching, will cause the arms and ammunition to be carefully examined, and will see that they are in *good order*. They will also be particularly careful that the men do not waste their cartridges. No muskets are to be carried in the wagons. One half of the fatigue party are to work at the same time; the other half are to carry the arms and accoutrements while on fatigue. The wagonmaster will attend to the loading of the wagons, and see that the different articles are put in good order, and that each wagon and team carry a reason able load. The hour of march is deferred until 9 o'clock , instead of 7. The officer of the day is charged with the execution of these orders.

The line of battle shall be formed agreeably to General Harrison's order on his late march to Fort Wayne.

James Winchester,
Brigadier-General.

26th. Two white men and Captain John (an Indian who was with us), lost their horses. They continued about the camping ground in search of them; they saw two or three Indians exploring our encampment. They took this method, no doubt, to calculate our number. The spies returned to camp this evening, who had discovered many Indian signs in front. Five of the spies who had yesterday started with the view to go to Fort Defiance, were found on the road shot, scalped, and tomahawked by the Indians or British.

27th. The spies and Captain Garrard's troop started this morning to bury the dead. They were attacked by a party of Indians who were watching the dead. One of the spies got shot in the ankle by an Indian. They fired on the Indians, and with the assistance of Captain Garrard, they made them run, but not without the loss of some of their savage blood. It was supposed some of them were badly wounded.

Captains Hickman and Ruddell returned, who had started this morning to reconnoitre Fort Defiance. They reported that they saw many fresh signs of Indians. As they returned to camp they spied an encampment of Indians; the Indians were talking and laughing merrily. A detachment was sent after dark in order to surprise them. Ruddell, their pilot, got lost before he got far, so that they could not execute their design.

28th. The army was alarmed about a mile from camp; we quickly paraded in order of battle, and were anxious to meet the enemy. The alarm proceeded from the spies, who fired at some Indians in front. The spies returned to camp this evening; they saw where a large number of Indians and British had encamped the night before.

29th. We continued on the same encampment, five miles from Defiance, and forty-five from Fort Wayne. The spies and horse troop were sent out in order to make discoveries. A party took the back track; they saw where the enemy had wheeled to the right about, and retreated; and fortunately for them they did so. Our industry in fortifying the camp with breastworks, and caution and vigilance with which it was guarded, would have rendered us able to have maintained our ground against a superior force. Wagon tracks were plainly to be seen—it was thought they were going to Fort Wayne with cannon, to take that place.

30th. We marched within one mile of Fort Defiance, and searched for a suitable place to encamp on: after every examination it was thought best to continue here, as it was a convenient place for timber. We pitched our tents and built very strong breastworks round the camp, which we had done for five or six nights past; we also slept with our guns in our arms, and paraded an hour before day, and stood under arms till nearly sunrise. From Fort Wayne to Defiance, we travelled on the north-west side of the Maumee River. The country is extremely level and well timbered, but badly watered.

Oct. 1. Colonel Lewis, with a detachment of three hundred and eighty men, started early this morning to pursue the Indians and British; they crossed the Auglaize River, and proceeded down the Maumee seven or eight miles, but could see nothing more than the appearance of the enemy retreating.

2nd. General Harrison arrived here with about one hundred mounted troops, and two days rations of flour. We have been without bread four days. We were informed General Harrison was appointed commander-in-chief of the North-Western Army; this was pleasing news to their troops, as he was the choice in preference to any other.

3rd. The troops that were with General Harrison, consisting of mounted riflemen and cavalry, three regiments, came to camp this morning from St. Mary's, which is sixty-three miles from Defiance. They came with speed, to assist the troops commanded by General Winchester. General Harrison had received information that all the British and Indian forces of Upper Canada were on their way to meet General Winchester at Defiance.

4th. There has been great murmuring in camp on account of the scarcity of provisions, which threatened a dissolution of this army. General Harrison having paraded the army, addressed them and said: there were twenty-five thousand rations provided for this army at St. Mary's; this should be conveyed here as soon as possible, part of which would be here today; he stated the con sequence of such mutinous complaints, and if this army would disperse, where could he get men who would stand? He said every exertion for the supply of this army with provisions and clothing, should be used. He informed us there would be a number of troops from Pennsylvania and Virginia to join us, amounting in all to ten thousand.

5th. A fatigue party of two hundred and forty men were employed to rebuild Fort Defiance. There were a few men on the other side of the river opposite to the fort. They discovered a party of Indians, twenty or thirty in number; they took them to be those friendly Indians who were with us; being not on their guard, they got close to them. Four or five of the Indians fired at the same time; they killed and scalped one of the men, and made their escape. The murder was committed not more than three hundred yards from the encampment of the mounted riflemen and cavalry, with General Tupper at the head of them. Those murderers were pursued immediately by two hundred horsemen; they pursued them in scattered order. A small party overtook them five or six miles from camp, and finding the enemy's force superior they had to retreat.

7th. The principal part of the clothing which was left at Piqua, came to camp; it has been greatly needed. A majority of the mounted men who were ordered to the rapids, and drew ten days provisions for *that expedition,* refused to march under General Tupper; of course the contemplated expedition failed, and they returned home, as their thirty days were nearly expired.

9th. A few days ago, Frederick Jacoby, belonging to the 17th regiment of United States infantry, was tried by a court-martial for sleeping on his post—he was condemned to be shot. The troops paraded and formed in a hollow square in close order, where the Rev. Mr. Shannon delivered a short discourse on the occasion. The square was then displayed, so that the army might witness the awful example of execution. The criminal was marched from the provost guard with solemn music, under a guard of a subaltern, sergeant, corporal, and twenty privates, to the place of execution; there he was blindfolded; the guard stood a few steps from him waiting the hour of execution. This was a solemn scene; a profound silence was kept by all the troops. But fortunately for the criminal, a reprieve arrived for him, just before the time of execution! The general judged him not a man of sound mind.

The spies reported they had killed an Indian, but could not get his scalp on account of other Indians; they stated there must be a large body of Indians near, by their trails.

10th. In consequence of the above report of the spies, Colonel Wells started with five hundred men in pursuit of the Indians; he pursued their trails twelve or thirteen miles, but could not see an Indian.

11th. The general ordered we should move and encamp near where the fort was building; this was, however, prevented by the inclemency of the weather; it rained and the wind blew all day, which made our situation very unpleasant. A man died in camp last night; he was buried with the honours of war; he was escorted to the grave in solemn order, and, after a short discourse by the Rev. Mr. Mitchell, six men fired three rounds over the grave; this was the first scene of the kind witnessed in our camp.

14th. We moved to the fort, and received a supply of provisions (salt, flour, and whiskey); we had been without salt ever since the 7th, and without flour two days.

16th. A detachment of one hundred men was sent this morning six miles below the fort, to a suitable place of timber to build pirogues.

18th. (Sunday.) The troops marched to the centre, agree ably to a general order, to hear the Rev. Mr. Shannon preach a sermon suited to the times. While he was zealously engaged there were six or seven guns fired down the river in quick succession; this alarmed the whole congregation—everyone flew to his arms and left the speaker alone. The alarm originated from a pirogue party, who had just arrived with a pirogue for a supply of provisions.

19th. The fort was finished and christened "Fort Winchester." It is composed of four blockhouses, a hospital and store house, and picketed between each blockhouse, containing about a quarter of an acre.

20th. The general issued an order for the troops to be assembled every morning at 9 o'clock , at such places near the encampment, as the commanding officers might deem convenient, and cause the rolls to be called, and mark all delinquents; and there, until 12 o'clock , practice the manual exercise, and man oeuvre according to Smith's instructions for infantry.

27th. In consequence of General Winchester's receiving information, he issued an order respecting clothing, which will show a flattering prospect of being supplied, an extract of which is as follows:—

General Orders. Fort Winchester, Oct. 27, 1812.

With great pleasure the general announces to the army the prospect of an early supply of winter clothing, amongst which are the following articles exported from Philadelphia on the 9th of September last, *viz.* 10,000 pairs of shoes, 5,000 blankets, 5,000 round jackets, 5,000 pairs of pantaloons, woollen cloth, to be made and forwarded to the westward immediately; besides the winter clothing for Colonel Wells's regiment some days before; 1,000 watch-coats, ordered from Philadelphia the 7th of October, 1812. September 24th, 5,000 blankets and 1,000 yards of flannel. 25th, 10,000 pairs of shoes. 29th, 10,000 pairs of woollen hose, 10,000 *do.* socks.

Yet a few days and the general consoles himself with the idea of seeing those whom he has the honour to command clad in warm woollen, capable of resisting the northern blasts of Canada.

J. Winchester,
Brigadier-General Commanding Left Wing N. W. Army.

29th. A fatigue party, consisting of three captains, three subalterns, three sergeants, three corporals, and one hundred and fifty privates was detached this morning, superintended by General Payne, to clear the way on the opposite side of the river, so as to make the view more extensive from the fort. The spies caught a prisoner fifteen or twenty miles below this place; he said he was just from Detroit; he was suspected as a spy, but he denied it; he said he deserted from the British, who had had him in confinement some time in consequence of his not taking the oath to be true to them.

Fort Winchester is situated near the point between the Maumee and Auglaize Rivers, and is a handsome place; it is predicted by some to become in a few years a populous city. The greater part of the land in the adjacent country is rich, and when improved will be equal, if not superior, to any in the western country. The Auglaize River empties into Great Miami, which runs a north course to Fort Winchester, and is navigable a considerable distance.

November 2. We moved across the River Maumee, opposite the point; it is a high piece of ground and very level, but in some degree wet and marshy: this movement was in order to get convenient to firewood.

3rd. This late place of encampment is found not to answer a good purpose; therefore the general thought it expedient to move from this to a piece of ground one-half mile lower down the river. As there were only a few wagons one regiment moved at a time—from twelve o'clock till after sunset before the last arrived at the place of destination. This last place appears to be very marshy, but not so much so as the former. It is very difficult to get a good place for an encampment at this time, as we have had several rainy days.

4th. The troops have been engaged in fortifying this late place of encampment with breastworks, so that we may be prepared for our enemies should they think proper to pay us a visit; the weather is very rainy, which makes our situation extremely un pleasant, though not more so than we could expect from the climate and season. Four of this army have gone to the silent tomb today, never more to visit their friends in Kentucky; the fever is very prevalent in camp; nearly every day there is one or more buried.

7th. We received information from Kentucky by passengers, of a quantity of clothing coming out for the volunteers. By every account from that quarter, the roads are almost impassable. Major Garrard and six of the spies started to the rapids this morning. This river abounds greatly with fish; large quantities have been caught with traps, and also with hooks and lines.

9th. Major Garrard and those men with him returned from the rapids. They made discoveries of a large quantity of corn, and some hogs and cattle, and a few Indians.

10th. The army moved six miles down the river, in order to be better accommodated with suitable ground for camping, and to build more pirogues. This encampment is the driest we have been at for some time; the land and timber are not inferior to any. I trust this country was designed for a more noble purpose than to be a harbour for those rapacious savages, whose manners and deportment are not more elevated than the ravenous beasts of the forest. I view the time not far distant, when this country will be interspersed with elegant farms and flourishing towns, and be in habited by a free and independent people, under an auspicious re public.

15th. A detachment of six captains, six subalterns, six sergeants, six corporals, and three hundred and eighty-six privates, started with six days provision, this morning, at reveille beating, to the rapids, under the command of Colonel Lewis.

17th. Colonel Lewis, with his detachment, returned about twelve o'clock , after a laborious march of sixty miles. About eighteen miles below this place, he was overtaken by an express from General Winchester, who had received intelligence of General Tupper, with five hundred men, being at the rapids, who had discovered a body of Indians, six or seven hundred in number, drinking and dancing. General Tupper, thinking this a good opportunity to attack them, attempted to cross the river, two miles above; he and two hundred of his men effected this, through great difficulty; in wading across some fell in the water and lost their guns, which discouraged the rest, so that General Tupper could not execute his design. This intelligence animated the troops commanded by Colonel Lewis, so that they wanted to continue on that night, without stopping, and attack the enemy before day. Colonel Lewis thought proper to halt, and send an express to General Tupper, for both parties to meet at Roche de Baut,[4] six miles above the Indian encampment, and unite their forces and surprise the enemy.

The express returned at three o'clock in the morning, and reported he had been at General Tupper's encampment, at the en trance of which he saw a man dead, scalped, and stripped. He concluded that General Tupper was defeated. This news changed the course of Colonel Lewis, not knowing their force. The general has thought proper to have this place strongly fortified with breastworks, four and a half feet high.

---

4. Pronounced Rushdeboo. (Roche de Boeuf. Original Ed.)

18th. One of the sentinels of the bullock guard discharged the contents of his gun at an Indian, as he thought, a few miles below camp, where the bullocks were grazing; the guard deserted the bullocks, and retreated to camp. A party was immediately sent in pursuit of the Indians, and behold! they found Michael Paul cutting a bee-tree.

20th. Ruddell returned, who was sent on the 17th to reconnoitre the rapids and Tupper's encampment. He discovered a large body of Indians at the rapids. He was through Tupper's encampment, where it was supposed he was defeated. He saw the man that was scalped and stripped, and he thought Tupper had retreated, instead of being defeated.

22nd. Smith and his party of spies had a little skirmish near Wolf town. Early in the morning they were eating their breakfasts; one of them started to get a drink of water; he had only got a few steps when an Indian fired and wounded him, but not mortally. After snapping twice, he fired and wounded an Indian. Several guns were fired by the Indians afterwards, but no injury was sustained. In returning to camp the wounded man was sent on some distance before, while part of them remained in the rear as a guard.

Captain Logan, Captain John, and another Indian, started to the rapids with the determination to establish their characters (for they were suspected by some to be traitors). Between this and the rapids, as they were rising a bank, they met seven Indians and a British officer, who took them prisoners, but let them carry their own guns. After taking them some considerable distance, they were determined to liberate themselves or fall a sacrifice. They succeeded in killing at the same time, the British officer[5] and two of the Indians; they stated Logan killed the second, but he got badly wounded through the body; one of the other Indians that were with him got wounded, but not mortally. The two wounded got on two horses that belonged to the dead and rode to camp, leaving Captain John to take scalps.

23rd. Captain John came in camp this morning with a scalp; he said it was the scalp of a Pottowatamie chief (Wynemack); he broke his knife in scalping him, which prevented him from scalping the others.

24th. Logan died, and was much lamented by the men generally, believing him to be true to the United States, and a brave soldier.

---

5. We learned since, the British officer was Colonel Elliott's son, and was probably a captain.

December 1. The troops are engaged in building huts, which are far preferable to tents.

2nd. The general has issued an order for the camp to be picketed, which is three-quarters of a mile round. It is on the north side of the river, and is composed of three lines. Colonel Wells's regiment on the right, Colonel Scott's, Lewis's, and part of Allen's in front, the remaining part of Allen's on the left, the river in the rear. The pickets were nearly completed in one day, two feet in the ground and eight feet above.

10th. The general has given orders to the commanding officers of regiments to cause each of their companies to be provided with a good pirogue sufficient to carry its own baggage, and cause all those who are without shoes to make themselves *moccasins* out of green hides.

There are many who have not shoes and clothes sufficient to keep them from freezing, should we move from here while they are in this condition; the clothes that the general flattered us with the expectation, and the clothes subscribed by the Kentuckians being not yet received, except a small part of the latter.

13th. Smith and his party returned from the rapids, who started two days ago in a canoe; they did not go far before they left the canoe, on account of the ice, and travelled by land; some of them were dangerously frostbitten.

14th. An express arrived in camp, certifying that the boats which started from St. Mary's on the 4th laden with flour and clothing, were frozen up in St. Mary's River, and the escort was building a house to store the loading in.

15th. Captain Hickman started this morning to forward flour and clothing immediately on packhorses.

16th. We have drawn no flour since the 10th, in consequence of which there was a letter handed to the general last night secretly, which stated that the volunteers in two days, except flour came before that time, would start and go to it; and they would carry their camp equipage to the fort if the general required it. This news was soon circulated through camp. The officers used every argument to suppress the appearance of a mutiny. A court-martial was held at Captain Williams's marquee to try John Hoggard, a private in Captain Price's company, for some misdemeanour. He was condemned to be drummed out of camp. Colonel Lewis paraded his regiment, and had him escorted with the fife and drum from one end of his line to the other. So he was legally discharged from the army. The most common punishment in camp for criminals is that of riding the wooden horse, or being put under guard on half rations. All the beef and pork was issued to the troops this evening; our dependence for the next ration is on a drove of hogs that has been expected several days!

17th. Three hundred head of hogs arrived to our relief.

20th. The weather is excessively cold; the ice has stopped the navigation of the river, so that the plan of going to the rapids by water is entirely frustrated; we had prepared about sixty pirogues for the voyage, which will be left here for our successors.

21st. The general has ordered the commandants of regiments to cause each company to be provided with a sufficient number of sleds to convey their baggage to the rapids. It is said these sleds are to be pulled by the men, as we have not a horse in camp able to pull an empty sled.

22nd. A little flour came to camp once more; quarter-rations of that article were issued, which was welcomed by rejoicing throughout camp.

24th. Captain Hickman returned with joyful news—that we should in a short time be supplied with flour. The deficiency of this article had produced serious consequences in the army. We have here been exposed to numberless difficulties, as well as deprived of the common necessaries of life; and what made these things operate more severely was, all hopes of obtaining any con quest was entirely abandoned. Obstacles had emerged in the path to victory, which must have appeared insurmountable to every person endowed with common sense. The distance to Canada, the unpreparedness of the army, the scarcity of provisions and the badness of the weather, show that Malden cannot be taken in the remaining part of our time. And would it not have been better if this army had been disbanded?

Our sufferings at this place have been greater than if we had been in a severe battle. More than one hundred lives have been lost, owing to our bad accommodations. The sufferings of about three hundred sick at a time, who are exposed to the cold ground and deprived of every nourishment, are sufficient proofs of our wretched condition. The camp has become a loathsome place. The hope of being one day relieved from these unnecessary sufferings affords some relief. We received this evening a supply of flour, and have been delivered from a state of starvation. It being Christmas eve, just after dark, a number of the guns were fired in quick succession; the whole army was ordered to parade in order of battle; strict orders were given to suppress the firing. About an hour before day the firing commenced again; the army was again paraded and strict orders given, threatening to punish the offenders.

27th. Part of the clothing arrived from Kentucky.

29th. We are now about commencing one of the most serious marches ever performed by the Americans. Destitute, in a measure, of clothes, shoes and provisions, the most essential articles necessary for the existence and preservation of the human species in this world, and more particularly in this cold climate. Three sleds are prepared for each company, each to be pulled by a pack-horse which has been without food for two weeks, except brush, and will not be better fed while in our service; probably the most of these horses never had harness on, but the presumption is they will be too tame; we have prepared harness out of green hides.

30th. After nearly three months preparation for this expedition, we commenced our march in great splendour; our elegant equipage cast a brilliant lustre on the surrounding objects as it passed! Our clothes and blankets looked as if they had never been acquainted with water, but intimately with dirt, smoke and soot; in fact, we have become acquainted with one much despised in Kentucky, under whose government we are obliged to live, whose name is *Poverty*. We marched six miles and encamped near Colonel Wells's regiment, which marched yesterday; the sick were left at No. Third, with a company from each regiment as a guard.

January 10. We arrived at Hull's road at the rapids, fifty miles from Fort Defiance, and encamped on a very high and suitable piece of ground. The second day after we left No. Third, the snow melted and the ground thawed, which operated much against our march. We marched two miles, which tried the strength and activity of our noble steeds. The general, who remained behind at No. Third, more properly styled Fort Starvation, thinking probably to take the advantage of the weather (this moderate thaw had opened the river in a ripple opposite to No. Third), had several pirogues loaded with his baggage, and manned immediately.

After travelling three or four hundred yards, they found that they were blockaded with ice; they landed and guarded the plunder, until arrangements could be made for its transportation by land. The weather took a change the second of January. It commenced snowing, and continued two days and nights: after it ceased, it was from twenty to twenty-four inches deep.

During this time we remained stationary. On the third the army resumed its march, wading through a deep snow. We had to stop early in the afternoon to prepare our encampment; to rake the snow away, make fires, and pitch our tents, was no trifling task; and after this we had to get bark or bushes to lie on; the linn,[6] in this case, was of great service to us. Many of the horses gave out and sleds broke down; consequently the plunder had to be pulled or carried by the men. I have seen six Kentuckians substituted instead of a horse, pulling their plunder, drudging along through the snow and keeping pace with the foremost.

In marching to this place we came through some good land, particularly the river bottoms, which are very rich. Wolftown, which is about half way between Fort Defiance and the rapids, is a handsome situation. This has formerly been an Indian town. We reached Roche De Baut the 9th, four miles above Hull's road, a place where some French had formerly lived. Early next morning (as cold a morning as the Kentuckians ever experienced) a detached party of six hundred and seventy-six men marched in front of the baggage, and went on four miles below the foot of the rapids, in order to examine if it were true, as said by some passengers from the right wing of the army, that there were six hundred Indians encamped and picketed in, six miles below the rapids. The detachment marched within two miles of the place, and sent spies, but they discovered no signs of Indians. The party remained all night, and partook of an elegant supper of parched corn, and returned to camp in the morning.

11th. Some fresh signs of Indians were seen near this encampment. A detachment of twenty-four men was sent immediately, under the command of Captain Williams. They had not got far before they discovered the Indians; the firing commenced on both sides nearly at the same time. The Indians stood but a little time before they ran, but not

---

6. Linn—or Lynn—is the bark of the *Tillia Americana*—the American Linden, which is easily peeled from the wood in large pieces (Original Ed.)

until they lost some of their savage blood. Captain Williams pursued them some miles, but could not overtake them. By the signs of blood, some of them must have been badly wounded. They left behind them two of their horses, a brass kettle, and some other plunder. One of Captain Williams's men received a wound in the arm, and another got shot through his hat. Captain Edmiston, who was one of the party, got his gun shot through the breech.

13th. Two Frenchmen came in camp last night from the River Raisin, who received information of the army being here by those Indians that Captain Williams pursued, who got there the night after the skirmish, and stopped only a few minutes, and then went on to Malden. Those Frenchmen solicited protection and assistance, stating the abuse they had received from the Indians, and the danger they were in of losing their lives and property.

25th. Arrived in camp this morning, clothing from Kentucky. The ladies who sent this clothing deserve the highest encomiums. If it had not been for their unexampled exertions, we must have suffered beyond conception. May they long live under the auspicious protection of a free government, and may kind heaven re ward their unparalleled benevolence!

Another Frenchman came to camp, confirming what was stated by the others. We now began to recruit after our laborious march, and after being deprived of a sufficiency of provisions. Although we have been without flour ever since we came here, yet we have been better supplied with provisions than we have been since we embarked in the service. We have here in possession many large fields of corn, probably three hundred acres. We have erected a great many pounding machines, to prepare it for our use. This place has a solemn appearance. The inhabitants have fled, and the Indians or British have burned their houses, leaving some of the chimneys standing. By every appearance, this has been a respectable settlement. Four miles below our encampment, are the remains of the old British garrison.

17th. A Frenchman came yesterday from the River Raisin; he said two companies of British had just arrived from Canada, and the Indians were collecting, and intended to burn Frenchtown in a few days. By the repeated solicitations of the French, and being counselled by some of the field officers, the general has been induced to order out a detachment of five hundred and seventy men, destined to the River Raisin; it was said, contrary to the instructions of General Harrison. The detachment started[7] early with three days provisions, and proceeded on twenty miles near to Presqu' Isle, a French village on the south side of the Maumee River. The sight of this village filled each heart with emotions of cheerfulness and joy; for we had been nearly five months in the wilderness, exposed to every inconvenience, and excluded from everything that had the appearance of a civilized country.

When the inhabitants of the village discovered us, they met us with a white flag, and expressed particular friendship for us. They informed us the British and Indians had left Frenchtown a few days ago, and had gone to Brownstown. About three hours after dark, a reinforcement of one hundred and ten men overtook us, commanded by Colonel Allen. Sometime in the latter part of the night an express came from the River Raisin, informing Colonel Lewis there were four hundred Indians and two companies of British there, and that Colonel Elliott was to start the next morning from Malden with a reinforcement.

18th. We started early, in order to get there before Colonel Elliott; after travelling fifteen miles, mostly on the ice, we received information of the enemy being there waiting for us; we were then within three miles of Frenchtown; we proceeded on with no other view than *to conquer or die.* When we advanced in sight of the town, and were about a quarter of a mile from it, the British saluted us by the firing of a piece of cannon; they fired it three times, but no injury was sustained. During this time we formed the line of battle, and, raising a shout,[8] advanced on them briskly; they soon commenced the firing of their small arms, but this did not deter us from a charge; we advanced close and let loose on them; they gave way, and we soon had possession of the village without the loss of a man! Three were slightly wounded. Twelve of their warriors were slain and scalped, and one prisoner taken before they got to the woods. In retreating they kept up some firing. We pursued them half a mile to the woods, which

---

7. The French, who were looking at us when we started, were heard to say we were not men enough.

8. A Frenchman who lived in this village said when the word came the Americans were in sight, there was an old Indian smoking at his fireside; the Indian exclaimed, "*Ho, de Mericans come, I suppose Ohio men come, we give them another chase;*" (alluding to the time they chased General Tapper from the rapids). He walked to the door smoking, apparently very unconcerned, and looked at us till we formed the line of battle, and rushed on them with a mighty shout! he then called out "*Kentuck, by G—d!*" and picked up his gun and ran to the woods like a wild beast.

111

were very brushy and suited to their mode of fighting.

As we advanced they were fixing themselves behind logs, trees, &c. to the best advantage; our troops rushed on them resolutely, and gave them Indian play, took the advantage of trees &c. and kept them retreating a mile and a half in the woods. During this time a heavy fire was kept up on both sides; at length, after a battle of three hours and five minutes, we were obliged to stop the pursuit on account of the approach of night, and retire to the village; we collected our wounded and carried them to the village, leaving our dead on the ground. In this action the Kentuckians displayed great bravery, after being much fatigued with marching on the ice; cowardice was entirely discountenanced; each was anxious to excel his fellow-soldiers in avenging his injured country; those only fell in the rear who were most fatigued.

Our loss in this action was eleven killed and fifty wounded.[9] Although the enemy had the advantage of the village in the first attack, and of the woods in the second, their loss, by the best information, far exceeded ours. A Frenchman stated they had fifty-four killed and a hundred and forty wounded, part of whom were carried to his house, on Sand Creek, a few miles from the village. An express and the Indian prisoner were sent immediately to the rapids. Some dispute arose between the Indians and some of the French on Sand Creek; the Indians killed an old man and his wife; in consequence of this the French were enraged, and resolved to get revenge. They applied to us for assistance, but it was thought improper to leave the village, though some of them had assisted us and fought in the front of the battle.

19th. A party was sent out to the battle-ground to bring in the dead, which were found scalped and stripped except one. In going over the battle-ground, great signs were seen (by the blood and where they had been dragged through the snow) of a considerable loss on the part of the enemy. Two of the wounded died. The British left a considerable quantity of provisions and some store goods, which answered us a valuable purpose. The wounded could have been as well accommodated here with every necessary as in any part of Kentucky. Apples, cider, sugar, butter and whiskey appeared to be plenty. The River Raisin runs an east course through a level country, interspersed with well-improved farms, and is seventy or eighty yards wide; the banks are low. Frenchtown is situated on the north side of this river,

9. It would have been better for us if we had been contented with the possession of the village, without pursuing them to the woods.

not more than three miles from the place it empties into Lake Erie. There is a row of dwelling-houses, about twenty in number, principally frame, near the bank, surrounded with a fence made in the form of picketing, with split timber, from four to five feet high; this was not designed as a fortification, but to secure their yards and gardens.

21st. A reinforcement of two hundred and thirty men arrived in the afternoon; also General Winchester, Colonel Wells, Major M'Clanahan, Captain Hart, Surgeons Irvin and Montgomery and some other gentlemen, who came to eat apples and drink cider, having been deprived of every kind of spirits nearly two months. The officers having viewed and laid off a piece of ground for a camp and breastworks, resolved that it was too late to remove and erect fortifications that evening; farther, as they resolved to remove early next day, it was not thought worthwhile, though materials were at hand, to fortify the right wing, which therefore encamped in the open field,[10] and Colonel Wells, their commander, set out for the rapids late in the evening.

A French man arrived here late in the evening from Malden, and stated that a large number of Indians and British were coming on the ice with artillery to attack us; he judged their number to be three thousand; he was not believed by some of our leading men, who were regaling themselves with whiskey and loaf sugar; but the generality of the troops put great confidence in the Frenchman's report, and expected some fatal disaster to befall us; principally because General Winchester had taken up his headquarters nearly half a mile from any part of the encampment, and because the right wing was exposed.

Ensign Harrow was sent with a party of men, sometime after night, by the orders of Colonel Lewis, to bring in all the men, either officers or privates, that he might find out of their quarters. After finding some and giving them their orders, he went to a brick house, about a mile up the river, and entered a room; finding it not occupied, he immediately went above stairs and saw two men, whom he took to be British officers, talking with the landlord. The landlord asked him to walk down into a stove room, and handing his bottle, asked him to drink, and informed him "there was no danger, for the British had not a force sufficient to whip us."

So Harrow returned about 1 o'clock and reported to Colonel Lewis what he had seen. Colonel Lewis treated the report with coolness, thinking the persons seen were only some gentle men from

---

10. This want of precaution was a great cause of our mournful defeat.

town; just at daybreak the *reveillé* began to beat, as usual; this gave joy to the troops, who had passed the night under the apprehensions of being attacked before day. The *reveillé* had not been beating more than two minutes before the sentinels fired three guns in quick succession; this alarmed our troops, who quickly formed and were ready for the enemy before they were near enough to do execution.

The British immediately discharged their artillery, loaded with balls, bombs, and grape-shot, which did little injury; they then attempted to make a charge on those in the pickets, but were repulsed with great loss. Those on the right being less secure for the want of fortification, were overpowered by a superior force, and were ordered to retreat to a more advantageous piece of ground. They got in disorder and could not be formed.[11] The Indians pursued them from all quarters, and surrounded, killed, and took the most of them. The enemy again charged on the left with redoubled vigour, but were again forced to retire.

Our men lay close behind the picketing, through which they had portholes, and everyone having a rest took sight, that his ammunition might not be spent in vain. After a long and bloody contest, the enemy finding they could not, either by stratagem or force, drive us from our fortification, retired to the woods, leaving their dead on the ground, except a party that kept two pieces of cannon in play on our right. A sleigh was seen three or four hundred yards from our lines going towards the right, supposed to be laden with ammunition to supply the cannon. Four or five men rose up and fired at once, and killed the man and wounded the horse. Some Indians who were hid behind houses continued to annoy us with scattering balls. At this time bread from the commissary's house was handed round among our troops, who sat composedly eating and watching the enemy at the same time.

Being thus refreshed, we discovered a white flag advancing toward us; it was generally supposed to be for a cessation of arms that our enemies might carry off their dead, which were numerous, although they had been bearing away both dead and wounded during the action; but how were we surprised and mortified when we heard that General Winchester, with Colonel Lewis had been taken prisoners by the Indians in attempting to rally the right wing, and that General

---

11. When the right wing began to retreat, it is said orders were given by some of the officers to the men in the eastern end of the picketing to march out to their assistance. Capt. Price and a number of men sallied out. Captain Price was killed, and most of the men.

Winchester had surrendered us prisoners of war to Colonel Proctor! Major Madison, then the highest in command, did not agree to this until Colonel Proctor had promised[12] that the prisoners should be protected from the Indians, the wounded taken care of, the dead collected and buried and private property respected.

It was then with extreme reluctance our troops accepted this proposition; there was scarcely a person that could refrain from shedding tears. Some plead with the officers not to surrender, saying they would rather die on the field. We had only five killed, and twenty-five or thirty wounded, inside of the pickets. The British asked, when they came in, what we had done with our dead, as they saw but few on the ground. A barn being set on fire to drive the Indians from behind it, they concluded that to conceal our dead, we had thrown them into these flames.

One of the houses that the wounded were in was much shattered by the cannon balls, though only a few struck as low as a man's head. The bombs flew over. Some bursted fifty feet above the ice, some fell on the ice, and some fell over the river. Notwithstanding all their exertions, their six cannon (which were all said to be six-pounders) did but little damage.

In this battle officers and privates exhibited the utmost firmness and bravery. Whilst the men were at their posts firing on the enemy, the officers were passing along the lines supplying them with cartridges. Major Graves, in passing around the line, was wounded in the knee. He sat down in a tent, bound up his wound, and cried: "Boys, I am wounded; never mind me, but fight on!"

The British collected their troops and marched in front of the village. We marched out and grounded our arms, in heat and bitterness

---

12. Colonel Proctor had informed General Winchester he would afford him an opportunity of surrendering his troops, and if not accepted he would let loose the Indians on us, who would burn the town, and he would not be accountable for their conduct. General Winchester, not knowing how we had resisted their efforts, thought probably it would be the case. But why did not Colonel Proctor make this proposition before he had exerted all his skill in trying to burn the town and to set the Indians on us? Proctor knew very well he had done all that was in his power with the force he had then, and he was then less able to rout us from the town than he was at first. The British informed us afterwards that Colonel Proctor had ordered a general retreat to Malden, and that they had *spiked four pieces of their cannon!* but he thought he would demand a surrender, according to custom. Our officers, knowing that we had but little ammunition, and the troops being still exposed to the fire of the cannon, thought proper to surrender.

of spirit. The British and Indians took possession of them. But all the swords, dirks, tomahawks, and knives were given up with promise that they should be restored again.[13]

All the prisoners, except those that were badly wounded, Dr. Todd, Dr. Bowers, and a few attendants, were marched towards Malden. The British said, as they had a great many of their wounded to take to Malden that evening, it would be out of their power to take ours before morning, but they would leave a sufficient guard, so that they should not be interrupted by the Indians. You will presently see with what aggravating circumstances the breach of this promise was attended.

Brother Allen Darnell having been badly wounded in the right shoulder on the 18th, and I being appointed to attend on the wounded, I continued with them.

Before the British and prisoners marched the Indians ransacked the camp, and got all the plunder that was remaining namely, tents, kettles, buckets, pans, &c.; then coming amongst the wounded, greatly insulted them, and took some of their plunder. After they went out I bolted the door. They came again and broke it open with their tomahawks. I immediately applied to a British officer, and told him the Indians were interrupting the wounded. He turned round, and called to another officer to send the guard. The Indians at that time had plundered the commissary's house (which was near the house in which the wounded were) of everything they wanted, and piled rails against it and set them on fire: I, with the assistance of two British officers put it out.

One of the British officers (Major Rundels) inquired where the ammunition was. I told him if there was any, it was above stairs. We went up, but could find none. There was a large quantity of wheat in the loft; he said it was a pity it was there, for the Indians would burn the house. I apprehended by that, the town was to be burned, and began to lament our wretched condition. After we went downstairs, Rundels asked me how many we had killed and wounded on the 18th. I told him, but he very haughtily disputed it. I had the return in my pocket. He read it, but made no reply.

Those that remained of us being hungry, I applied to one of the British in the evening for some flour, as there were a good many barrels in the commissary's house, which I considered to be long to them. He told me to take as much as I wanted. I asked him if there was a guard left? He said there was no necessity for any, for the Indians were going to their camp, and there were interpreters left, who would walk

13. This promise was broken.

from house to house and see that we should not be interrupted. He kept walking about and looking towards the road. He told me I had better keep in the house, for the Indians would as soon shoot me as not, although he had just told me we should not be interrupted! I suspected he was looking for General Harrison. Oh! if we had seen General Harrison coming with his troops, the wounded would have leaped for joy! but I did not expect him.

As they did not leave the promised guard, I lost all confidence in them, and expected we would be all massacred before morning. I being the only person in this house not wounded, with the assistance of some of the wounded, I prepared something for about thirty to eat. The Indians kept searching about town till after dark. One came in the house who could talk English, and said he commanded a company after the retreating party, and that most of the party were slain. He said the men gave up their guns, plead for quarters, and offered them money if they would not kill them; but his boys, as he called them, would tomahawk them without distinction. He said the plan that was fixed on by the Indians and British, before the battle commenced, was that the British were to attack in front to induce us to charge on them; five hundred Indians were placed on the right hand and five hundred on the left, to flank round and take possession of the town; but he said we were too cunning for them, we would not move out of the pickets.

We passed this night under the most serious apprehensions of being massacred by the tomahawk or consumed in the flames. I frequently went out during the night to see if the house was set on fire. At length the long wished-for morn arrived, and filled each heart with a cheerful hope of being delivered from the cruelty of those merciless savages. We were making every preparation to be ready for the promised sleighs; but alas! instead of the sleighs, about an hour by sun a great number of savages, painted with various colours, came yelling in the most hideous manner! These bloodthirsty, terrific savages (sent here by their more cruel and perfidious allies, the British) rushed into the houses where the desponding wounded lay, and insolently stripped them of their blankets and all their best clothes, and ordered them out of the houses. I ran out of the house to inform the interpreters[14] what the Indians were doing. At the door, an Indian took my hat and put it on his own head. I then discovered the Indians had been at the other

---

14. I was since informed that Colonel Elliott instructed the interpreters to leave the wounded, after dark, to the mercy of the savages. They all went off, except one half-Indian.

house first, and had used the wounded in like manner.

As I turned to go back into the house, an Indian, taking hold of me, made signs for me to stand by the corner of the house. I made signs to him I wanted to go in and get my hat; for I desired to see what they had done with the wounded. The Indians sent in a boy who brought out a hat and threw it down to me, and I could not get in the house. Three Indians came up to me and pulled off my coat. My feeble powers cannot describe the dismal scenes here exhibited. I saw my fellow soldiers, naked and wounded, crawling out of the houses to avoid being consumed in the flames. Some that had not been able to turn themselves on their beds for four days, through fear of being burned to death, arose and walked out and about through the yard. Some cried for help, but there were none to help them. "Ah!" exclaimed numbers, in the anguish of their spirit, "what shall we do?"

A number, unable to get out, miserably perished in the unrelenting flames of the houses, kindled by the more unrelenting savages. Now the scenes of cruelty and murder we had been anticipating with dread during the last night, fully commenced. The savages rushed on the wounded, and in their barbarous manner, shot, and tomahawked and scalped them; and cruelly mangled their naked bodies while they lay agonizing and weltering in their blood. A number were taken towards Malden, but being unable to march with speed, were inhumanly massacred. The road was for miles strewed with the mangled bodies, and all of them were left like those slain in battle, on the 22nd, for birds and beasts to tear in pieces and devour. The Indians plundered the town of everything valuable, and set the best houses on fire.

The Indian who claimed me gave me a coat, and when he had got as much plunder as he could carry he ordered me, by signs, to march, which I did, with extreme reluctance, in company with three of the wounded and six or seven Indians. In travelling about a quarter of a mile, two of the wounded lagged behind about twenty yards. The Indians, turning round, shot one and scalped him. They shot at the other and missed him; he, running up to them, begged that they would not shoot him. He said he would keep up, and give them money. But these murderers were not moved with his doleful cries. They shot him down; and rushing on him in a crowd, scalped him.

In like manner my brother Allen perished. He marched with difficulty after the wounded, about two or three hundred yards, and was there barbarously murdered. My feelings at the sight and recollection of these inhuman butcheries cannot be described. In addition to these deep sorrows for the mournful fate of my companions, and the cruel death of a dear brother, I expected every moment, for a considerable time, that the same kind of cruelty and death would be my portion. The Indians that guarded me and one of the wounded, observing our consternation, one that could talk English said, "We will not shoot you." This a little revived our hopes, that were almost gone;[15] and he, having cut a piece, hide and all, of a dead cow, started. It is their common practice to kill a cow or hog, and take a piece and leave the rest. In travelling two miles, we came to a house where there were two British officers; the Indian made a halt, and I asked one of the officers what the Indian was going to do with me; he said he was going to take me to Amherstburg (or Malden). I judged these villains had instructed the Indians to do what they had done.

A few miles farther we came to the Indian encampment, where there were a great many hallooing and yelling in a hideous manner. I thought this my place of destiny. The Indian took off my pack, broiled a piece of meat and gave me part; this I ate merely in obedience to him. Then we started and arrived at Amherstburg, eighteen miles from Frenchtown. The other prisoners had just arrived. The British were firing their salute. The Indian took me into a house not far from the fort; it was probably their council house; it would have held five hundred. It was inhabited by a large number of squaws, children and dogs. They welcomed me by giving me some bread, meat and hominy to eat. After this an Indian asked me if I had a squaw; I told him not; he immediately turned round and talked to the squaws in Indian, while I sat in a pensive mood observing their motions.

I discovered the squaws were pleased, by their tittering and grinning; one, I observed, had a great desire to express her joy by showing her teeth; but the length of time she had lived in this world had put it out of her power. I suspected, from their manoeuvres, I would have to undergo a disagreeable adoption (as other prisoners had done) and,

---

15. Upon taking a view of these scenes of woe, who can avoid some such exclamation as the following? Why has the all-seeing, beneficent Ruler of the universe delivered so many of our choice officers and brave soldiers into the hands of our enemies, to be slain in battle and to lie unburied, to be dragged away in the galling chains of captivity, and to be put to torturing deaths by monsters of cruelty? Not, I presume, because of infidelity and injustice towards our enemies; but owing to our ingratitude towards the God of armies; and to our want of confidence in Jehovah our pride, our too great confidence in our own wisdom, valour, and strength; our unbelief and a catalogue of vices too tedious to enumerate. Aggravated national crimes have involved us in heavy and complicated judgments!

what was a task still more unpleasant, to be united in the conjugal band to one of these swarthy, disgustful animals. The Indian asked me a few questions—where we had come from—how far it was—when we started—and if there were any more coming. In reply to these questions, I gave him but little satisfaction. After this they spread blankets down, and made signs for me to go to bed. I did, and soon fell asleep, as I was much fatigued and had not slept much for four nights past. Early next morning, the Indian collected his family and all his property, and started: I knew not where he was going; he gave me a knapsack and gun to carry.

Now I despaired of getting with the other prisoners, unless I could desert from the Indians. I expected I would be taken to an Indian town, there to undergo a disagreeable adoption, or to be burned to death with firebrands. As he took me near Fort Malden, I took as good a view of it as I could while I passed it. It stands about thirty yards from the river bank. I judged it to be seventy or eighty yards square; the wall appeared to be built of timber and clay. The side from the river, was not walled, but had double pickets, and entrenched round about four feet deep; and in the entrenchment was the second row of pickets. As we went on through the edge of town (Amherstburg) I asked an Englishman where the other prisoners were. He said they were in town, in a wood-yard; the Indian hurried me along and would not let me talk to the Englishman. The Indian had a little horse, packed with his plunder, which I resolved to take, if possible, and ride into town that night.

He took me to his place of residence, about three miles from Malden. I was anxious for the approach of night, so that I might make my escape. While I was consoling myself with the anticipation of seeing my fellow sufferers at Malden, night made its approach. Sometime after dark the Indian spread blankets down, and made signs for me to lie down, and put my coat, shoes, and socks, under his own head. I wanted him to leave my socks on, for my feet would get cold; he made signs to warm them by the fire. Thus I was sadly disappointed.

Next day he examined all his plunder. He had a very good suit of clothes, besides several other coats, socks, shoes, &c.; among these were Wesley's Sermons and a great many papers, which he gave me to read. I found several old letters, but nothing of value. He discovered I wanted to shave, and got his razor, shaving-box and a piece of glass, and made signs for me to shave. After this I lay down on some blankets and fell asleep. He came and awoke me, and gave me a twist of tobacco, which I received as a token of friendship. In a short time after, he started to Malden, and made signs for me to stay there till he would come back.

He returned in the evening with a blanket, tied full of loaves of bread just out of the oven, besides some meat. The Indians always gave me a plenty to eat; and served me before any of the family, with more politeness than I expected to find amongst them. He had drawn some money. I asked him to let me look at it. I found it to be pieces of cards with the number of *livres*[16] written on them.

The third night at length arrived; and he made my bed as usual and took my coat and shoes, but accidentally left my socks on. I lay down with the determination to leave him before morning. I slept very well for awhile. When I awoke, the house was dark. I thought this as good an opportunity of deserting as I could get, but with considerable timidity I made the attempt. I crawled to the door very easily, and raised the blanket that hung up at the door; just as I was going out he coughed, and I stopped until I thought he was asleep, and then started, without shoes or coat, to Amherstburg. When I got there, I examined several yards and gardens to see if there was any fire. After going through many streets I turned my course towards the river, and accidentally came to the house where the prisoners were. The sentinel, who was standing at the door, let me in without much ceremony. Providence smiled on this attempt to extricate myself from the Indians. Thus, through mercy, I escaped from the savages, and was delivered from the doleful apprehensions of being sacrificed in some barbarous and cruel manner, to gratify their bloodthirsty souls. I got in between two of my comrades who were lying next to the door. My feet were almost frozen before morning.

During my captivity with the Indians, the other prisoners were treated very inhumanly. The first night, they were put in a wood-yard; the rain commenced early in the night, and put out all their fires. In this manner they passed a tedious night, wet, and benumbed with cold. From this place they were taken to a cold warehouse, still deprived of fire, with their clothes and blankets frozen, and nothing to eat but a little bread. In this wretched condition they continued two days and three nights!

26th. The Indians came early in the morning to search for me, but they were not admitted into the house. The guard said it would be

16. This was the device used by the early French governors of Canada (Original Ed.)

well for me to keep as much concealed as possible, for if the Indian I had left could get me he would kill me. He came to the door, and made motions to show how he would scalp me. I disguised myself by changing my clothes and tying up my head, so that he did not know me. The prisoners being destined to Fort George were divided in two divisions, the first to keep a day's march before the second, in order probably, to be better supplied with provisions on the way.

I being attached to the first division, the Indians examined the lines very closely for me, but not possessing discernment sufficient to know me I fortunately escaped. Malden, or Amherstburg, is situated on the east side of Detroit River, near its junction with Lake Erie, and contains about one hundred houses, mostly frame; in lat. 42° 22' N., long. 8° 3' W. from Philadelphia.

We set out from this town and marched seventeen miles to Sandwich, a small town on the east side of Detroit River, and one mile below Detroit; it contains perhaps about three hundred in habitants. We were divided in small companies, and put into different houses, where we had the happiness once more to see fire.

27th. We drew a ration of bread and fresh beef, but no salt, and had no way of cooking the beef. We commenced our march at 1 o'clock , and marched ten miles, part of the way on Lake St. Clair. In the evening we were conducted to cold barns and there shut up till morning, deprived of fire.

28th. We recommenced our march early, as cold a morning as ever I experienced, and continued twenty-four miles on Lake St. Clair; at night we were conducted to a cold barn on the beach; we lay without fire, except a few who could not get in, who had the happiness of encamping in the woods.

29th. We again resumed our march, and continued on the lake fifteen miles to the mouth of La Tranche River, called by some the River Thames; during this time we had to run to keep ourselves from freezing; we continued up the river five miles, and stopped while the guard went in to warm and to get their dinner. Having drawn no provisions since we left Sandwich, some of the prisoners were driven to the necessity of picking up frozen potatoes and apple peelings that had been thrown out in the yard. One of the prisoners, being unable to keep pace with the rest, was left on the lake, but was accidentally overtaken by a sleigh and brought on.

After being in a stove room sometime, he was led out to march, trembling with cold. One of the guard observed, "he was a man of no spirit to freeze such a day as this." So barbarous were their dispositions and treatment, that I concluded we should die of cold and hunger. We marched ten miles farther to Captain Dolson's, where we were conducted into a large still-house. A number lodged below among the still-tubs by the fire; the rest on the loft, where they were annoyed with the smoke. Sometime in the night they brought us a little bread and meat.

30th. We drew two days provisions, and cooked it.

31st. It snowed all day; notwithstanding, we marched twenty-four miles and were shut up in a barn wet and cold. Going to a barn to lodge so cold an evening was like approaching a formidable enemy, for we expected to perish with cold in the dreary dwelling. Many got their feet frostbitten. We tried in vain to keep our shoes from freezing by putting them under our heads.

February 1. We continued our march twenty-two miles in a thinly settled country, and passed through the Moravian nation of Indians; in the evening we encamped in the woods.

2nd. We marched twenty-two miles, suffering greatly both with hunger and cold. In the evening w r e arrived at Delaware township, a small settlement on the River La Tranche. We were divided into small companies, and were permitted to lodge in houses by fires.

3rd. We had been two days without provisions. Here we drew rations for three days. Captain Dolson left us today; the prisoners must forever detest his baseness and cruelty. We resumed our march in the evening and continued five miles, notwithstanding the snow was two feet deep, and it was then snowing. We were better treated by our new guard.

4th. We marched twenty-six miles to the head waters of the River Thames, to Oxford township, a settlement of ten or twelve miles in length.

5th. We marched two miles, and were detained for a supply of provisions.[17] After being supplied we continued our march in the evening

17. Here we met a number of the 41st regiment of British regulars, just from Fort George, going to Malden to supply the places of those who were killed on the 2nd of January, at Frenchtown. They appeared to be very sociable, generally of the Irish descent. One of their officers said "in a few weeks they would drive General Harrison and all his army along there" Yes," replied James Allen (who was one of my messmates), "before that time your Irish hides will be riddled, (continued next page),

three miles farther, and where we lodged were treated very civilly by the inhabitants.

6th. After marching twenty-four miles, principally through a wilderness, we arrived at Burford township.(See note following)

Note:—Six of us, who formed, a mess, stopped at a Major Boon's and asked him "if we might stay all night." He said we could. His father, who lived with him, let us know he had been a Tory Major in the American revolution. He said "he had lived in the Jerseys, and had one of Lord Howe's commissions in the house then, and was a half-pay officer." He said "the Americans would have no possible chance to take Canada, for the British next spring would bring seventy thousand Indians from the north-west, and as many negroes from St. Domingo, besides three hundred thousand Turks!"

Said James Allen, "I suppose you will set dogs on us next!"

The old fellow said "it was very evident the Lord was on their side!"

Then said Allen, "If the Lord has joined with the British, savages, and negroes, to massacre his own people, it is surprising! But I rather think it is only your Canadian lord that acts in this manner." The old fellow then ordered him out of the house. He told him "he was very well suited in a room, and would stay till morning." They still continued arguing.

The old fellow said "We had no business on their soil," alluding to Frenchtown. Allen told him "we were on our own soil." He said "it was a lie, for Michigan Territory was given up to them by General Hull."

Said Allen, "Hull was such a fellow as the d——l, who offered Christ all the kingdoms of the world if he would fall down and worship him; when, poor old sneaking whelp, he did not own a foot on earth."

Said Boon, "You had better stayed away, for all you have done;

so that they would not hold hickory nuts." Another of that party said, what nonsensical things those leather stocks were which we wore, with the sign of the eagle pecking out the eyes of the lion. Said Allen, "This is only the shadow, the substance will soon follow." Note: James Allen is the same who fought in the duel with Fuller, near Fort Massac, who was supposed to be a British spy, before the commencement of the war. Fuller, after having been twice knocked down by Allen's balls, was found to have a Dutch blanket folded, and a quire of paper over his cowardly breast as a shield. Allen was not injured.

the major who commanded the Indians on the 18th was here a few nights ago, and said there was not one killed, and but three wounded."

Said Allen, "I would not believe my father if he were to tell me so, for I saw a number that were killed and scalped and lay on the snow for days; and if there were but three wounded, there must have been an abundance of blood in them to have stained the snow for miles square."

Said he, "Did you scalp them? you are bloody dogs."

"Yes," said Allen, "you might say so, if we had hired the savages to kill your women and children, and massacre and burn your wounded, when we had promised to take care of them."

He said "the British had never hired the Indians to kill women and children; they were too humane a people to do so."

"Yes," said Allen, "they showed humanity in the time of the American Revolution, when they paid the Indians for infants scalps that were taken out of their mothers' wombs; they call themselves Christians, and when the Indians sent home to them scalps, from the unborn infant to the gray hairs, in bales like goods, they had days of feasting, rejoicing, and thanksgiving to the Lord, for the victory they had gained the d——l would be ashamed to acknowledge such a people as any part of his offspring." The old fellow again ordered him out of the house; but Allen told him "he would go in the morning." Allen said "we had more friends in Canada than they had."

"Yes," said he, "there are men mean enough to join against their own country."

Allen replied, "none but a mean, low-lived wretch would fight against his own country."

The old fellow took the hint, as he had been a Tory, and got in a violent passion. He asked Allen "if he was not a Congressman?" Allen said "No."

"Are you an Assemblyman?"

"No."

"Are you a Yankee lawyer?"

"No."

"Well, you are a Yankee liar, then."

Allen said: "if we were of an age, and on an equal footing, you would not give me the lie so often." The old fellow told Allen "he must be an antediluvian, for he appeared to know all things that had passed, and all the crimes that England ever committed seemed to be fresh on his mind; he supposed he was one of the greatest enemies the British had."

Allen said "he had done his best; and if he was exchanged he would shoot at them as long as he could crook his finger to draw the trigger."

A young woman who was in the house said "we were only coming to drive them off their lands."

Allen said "we were only coming to set them free, so that those lands might be their own, and not King George's."

She said "the Americans that were killed at Queenstown had deeds in their pockets for all their best plantations."

Said Allen "I must believe it because you say so, but if I had seen it myself I would not."

The old fellow's passion subsided, and Allen and he were friendly.

7th. In marching thirty miles to a little village near the head of Lake Ontario, we passed through the Mohawk Nation of Indians on Grand River, who are much whiter than any we have seen; their mode of dress is not different from other Indian nations, and they have the same savage appearance; we were informed that there are six nations on this river who hold a large body of the best land.

8th. We drew our rations and proceeded on sixteen miles. In going down towards Lake Ontario, we descended a precipice up wards of two hundred feet into a level country; this precipice extends across Niagara River, and occasions those remarkable falls.

9th. We marched eighteen miles through a well-settled country.

10th. We marched sixteen miles to Newark, lately called Niagara West; it contains about five hundred inhabitants; many of the buildings are handsome, composed of brick and stone; it has several churches, an academy, six taverns, and about twenty stores; it is situated on the west side of Niagara River, in lat. 43° 15' N., long. 4° west; Fort George stands at the upper end of the town.

We continued here no longer than was necessary to make arrangements to cross the river. A British officer took down our names and the regiment and company we belonged to, and said "we must not take up arms against Great Britain and her allies until legally exchanged." Thus we were paroled; they hoisted a flag and took us across

Niagara River,[18] which is about one-quarter of a mile wide to Fort Niagara, which is situated at the junction of Niagara River and Lake Ontario, in New York State; it is strongly fortified, and well supplied with artillery.

A FEW REMARKS RESPECTING UPPER CANADA AND ITS INHABITANTS.

From Malden to Sandwich, and a considerable distance up St. Clair, resembles a level plain thickly interspersed with farms and houses; many places look like little villages. The houses are principally frame, and have an ancient appearance. Besides being well supplied with grain from their farms, they receive considerable benefit from their orchards.

The River La Tranche is a considerable navigable stream, and runs a westerly course into Lake St. Clair; the land near it is rich and fertile; the timber is oak, ash, hickory, walnut, sugar-tree, &c. It is thickly settled as far as Moraviantown; but, from the river on the north side, is an extensive wilderness of poor swampy land. From Moraviantown to Grand River is a wilderness of poor piney land, except Delaware, Oxford, and Burford town ships, which are tolerable settlements. From Grand River to Fort George is a rich, well-settled country, particularly along Lake Ontario.

The inhabitants are composed of English, French, Dutch, and a great many emigrants from the United States. The whole has been estimated at eighty thousand; besides these, there are unknown numbers of Indians. The Canadians are generally a well-looking people, remarkably fair, but not well informed. They do not set a great value on education, and it is not encouraged by the government. Although their laws appear to be moderate, yet neither the freedom of speech nor the freedom of the press is encouraged. The officers are haughty and tyrannical in the execution of their orders. I learned that a majori-

---

18. The second division, who had been used far better than the first, arrived the day following, and were paroled in like manner, amounting in all to five hundred and twelve. Particular inquiries were made respecting the British loss in the battle of the 22nd, while passing through Canada. The loyalists stated their loss to be very trifling; some would say fifteen killed, and others twenty-five. But different persons, in whom we had reason to place confidence, stated their loss to be very considerable about six hundred killed and wounded, and amongst these Colonel St. George. This account will not be considered exaggerated, when reflecting on the length of time they were exposed to a deliberate and well-directed fire from our troops... .the number that was seen lying on the ground after they retreated, and the number of sleighs loaded with their bloody guns.

ty[19] of the inhabitants were in favour of the United States government, and many had concealed themselves to avoid taking up arms.

The British forces consist of regulars, flankers, militia, Negroes, and Indians. Agreeably to an act of their assembly in 1812, their flankers are riflemen, volunteered or drafted for the term of six months, and longer if not then relieved. The militia cannot be called into service for more than twenty days, unless their country is invaded. I heard of two companies of Negroes, runaways from Kentucky, and other States, who are commanded by white men. A great many of the Indians are stationed near the lines, who can be called to arms at a minute's warning.

11th. After regaling ourselves on the plenty of food and drink afforded us in the land of liberty, we set our faces homewards. One mile from Niagara Fort, we came to Salt Battery; it was composed of barrels of salt and dirt. From this they could play upon Fort George. We proceeded up the river eight miles to Lewistown, which is on the east bank of Niagara River, opposite Queenstown, and contains only a few houses; eight miles farther, we came to Grand Niagara, a small village on the east bank of Niagara River just above the falls, and nearly opposite Chippeway. Above the falls, in the middle of the river, is an island about three hundred yards long, the lower end of which is just at the perpendicular edge of the fall. On both sides of this island, all the waters of the rivers and lakes to the north-west, fall down a precipice of one hundred and thirty-seven feet perpendicular, and fall near as much more in a rapid of nine miles below. Before the water comes to the fall, as it passes the island, it seems in swiftness to outfly an arrow.

12th. We arrived at Black Rock, nineteen miles above the falls. Here is a considerable village, a navy yard, and three batteries well furnished with cannon. It took its name from its rocky situation. From this we continued on two miles and a half to Buffalo, the capital of Buffalo county, New York State. It is situated at the foot of Lake Erie, opposite to Fort Erie.

We continued at Buffalo one day, on account of the badness of the weather, and then continued our march thirty-two miles on the lake,

---

19. An inhabitant near the head of Lake Ontario heard of the prisoners, and went to see them. He began to talk to one, judging him to be an American officer, and telling him he had more friends in Canada than the British had, and if he wanted money, or any assistance, he should be accommodated. The poor fellow soon found his mistake, that he was talking to a British officer, just from Fort George.

and then marched through a well-settled country to Erie, the county town of Erie County, in Pennsylvania. It is ninety miles from Buffalo, and is situated on the south-east shore of Lake Erie. We proceeded on by the way of Waterford and Meadville, one hundred and twenty miles, to Pittsburgh, and from Pittsburgh to Kentucky, by water.

Language fails to express the emotions I felt on arriving safely at home, to enjoy the caresses and society of dear friends, after having endured so much fatigue, and having been so often exposed to imminent danger; and having so frequently expected death, attended with *all the horrors of Indian cruelty.*

Narrative of Mr. Timothy Mallary

During the battle on the 22nd January, 1813, at Frenchtown, on the River Raisin, between the combined forces of British, Canadians, and Indians, and the American forces, I received a wound from a piece of plank, which had been split off by a cannon ball. It struck me on the side, and unfortunately broke three of my ribs. The battle having terminated in favour of the combined forces, and I not being able to travel with those American prisoners who were to march immediately for Malden, I remained on the ground until the next morning, with the rest of my wounded countrymen, who had received a solemn promise from the British commander, that they should be taken to Malden in sleighs.

This sacred promise was not regarded. It was sacrificed on the altar of savage barbarity! to the god of murder and cruelty! Instead of sleighs, Indians were sent prepared to murder these unfortunate victims, who, after they had executed in part their purpose on the ground where we lay, ordered several other prisoners and myself to march for Malden. We had not proceeded far before they tomahawked four of this number, amongst whom was Captain Hart, of Lexington. He had hired an Indian to take him to Malden. I saw part of this hire paid to the Indian.

After having taken him some distance, another Indian demanded him, saying that he was his prisoner; the hireling would not give him up; the claimant, finding that he could not get him alive, shot him in the left side with a pistol. Captain Hart still remained on his horse; the claimant then ran up, struck him with a tomahawk, pulled him off his horse, scalped him, and left him lying there.

We proceeded on until we came within three miles of Brownstown, where we encamped for the night. The next day we proceeded on to their encampment, seven or eight miles from Detroit, on the

River Rouge, which appeared to be headquarters. They were furnished at this place with bark *wigwams*; here was a large number of
squaws and children, I suppose two thousand.

They here stripped off my clothes, and dressed me after the Indian
manner. They shaved off my hair, except a small quantity on the top
of my head, which they left for the purpose of rendering the task of
scalping more easy. They bored my ears, which they supplied plenti-
fully with ear-rings, frequently by hanging one in another, like the
links of a chain. They wanted to bore my nose, but I objected, and
they did not insist. They frequently painted my face one-half black
and the other red, and frequently with red and black streaks.

Shortly after our arrival at these encampments, I was adopted into
a Pottowatomie family that had lost a son in the battle at the River
Raisin.

I was presented to this family by an Indian whose name was Ke-
wi-ex-kim. He introduced me to my father and mother, brothers and
sisters, and instructed me to call them by these respective appella-
tions. My father's name was Asa Chipsaw, after whom they call me;
they asked me if I had a squaw; I answered in the negative, at which
they appeared well pleased, and brought me a squaw, urging me to
marry her. I refused, and told them when I got well I would accede
to the proposals; this they took as a great offence. After having made
themselves acquainted with the situation of my wound, they made a
tea of *sassafras* and cherry-tree barks, which was the only drink I was
permitted to take for fifteen days.

They frequently took me to Detroit, for the purpose of helping
them to pack provisions from thence to their encampment. But they
would not suffer me to talk to the inhabitants of that place. Fifteen
loaves of bread, weighing three pounds each, ten pounds of pork or
beef, and a peck of corn, was what they drew for six days. This would
not last more than half that time; the remaining part they lived upon
fragments of dog or horse meat. They appeared indifferent whether
they had killed the animal that day themselves, or whether it had died
by some accidental cause seven or eight days prior to their eating it.

They appointed me cook. I then had to undergo much fatigue in
getting wood, &c., for they lent no assistance. Their customary way of
cooking is to boil the meat and make soup, which they immediately
devour without salt.

They have drunken frolics, whenever they can get any kind of
spirits to drink. When these frolics take place the squaws hid me, to

prevent them from murdering me. Once I was hid in some brush and deprived of food for four days, during which time there was a continual uproar in the camp, as though they had been killing each other.

The squaws, who frequently visited me, and to whom I as often applied for something to eat, informed me that there could be nothing had until the men got sober, who would then either kill provisions, or draw from Detroit. On the fourth day, when I had given up to perish, they brought me a piece of a dog cooked without salt, and although you may feel squeamish when I mention it, yet it was to me the sweetest morsel that I ever recollect to have eaten.

During my stay with them I saw them take a number of scalps to Malden, for which they said they received from four to six dollars each, either in whiskey or store goods. They said they got thirty-seven scalps at the battle of the 18th and upwards of four hundred at that of the 22nd January. I replied, that there were only ten scalped on the 18th. They said "Yankee d——d lie;" and they further stated, that they had only two killed on the 18th. I replied "Indian d——d lie," for I saw myself twelve dead on the field. I asked them how many British and Indians were at the River Raisin, on the 22nd January; they replied, that there were two thousand five hundred Indians, and one thousand British.

They would frequently make motions imitating the Americans when they were scalping them, by turning, twisting, mourning,[1] &c.; this was done to aggravate me.

They once gave me a jug of whiskey, requesting me to drink. I drank what satisfied me, and offered them the jug again—they insisted on me to drink more; I put the jug to my head, but did not drink; they discovered the cheat, and cried out "Yankee no good man, d——d lie;" they then made me drink until they could hear it gurgle in my throat.

About three weeks before the battle at the rapids the squaws and boys were employed in dressing deer-skins, which were to equip the warriors for their march thither. During this time, the warriors were collecting and dancing the war dance. They informed me that they were going to *Quo-by-ghaw*, which I learned from the French, was the rapids. I further learned that the British had promised them the possession of Fort Meigs, as well as the disposal of General Harrison. They then calculated on Fort Meigs as their chief place of deposit, from which they could make incursions into the State of Ohio, kill

1. Moaning.

a vast number of the inhabitants, and satisfy themselves with plunder. They calculated on having a three days' frolic in the burning of General Harrison.

Two weeks before their march for Fort Meigs Tecumseh was with them. He was busily employed rallying those who were in different about going to the battle, and encouraging those who had volunteered; amongst other persuasive arguments to volunteer, he made use of these, *viz*: that Fort Meigs was badly constructed and illy defended; asserting that they could take it without the loss of a man. But, if this could not be effected, he would then lead them on to Fort Wayne, which would certainly fall an easy prey to them. He then left them, and went to the Wabash to bring his warriors, who were stationed at that place.

Previous to the march of the Indians, they took bark of swamp willow, and tobacco, mixed them together, and pulverized them. They then formed a circle round a fire which had been prepared for that purpose, and one rose and delivered a speech, I understood, relative to the war. At the conclusion of the speech, they passed this powder around the circle, each individual taking a pinch as it passed; each then snuffed a part of this portion, and threw the remaining part in the fire. After this had been performed with the greatest solemnity, one took the snuff which yet remained in the vessel, and threw it in the fire. They then took up their packs, raised the scalp halloo, waved their tomahawks over their heads, and marched for battle.

There were three thousand who drew four days' rations at Detroit. When they left us, they told us to be good boys, and stay there till they came back, and they would bring some more Yankees, who should cook and do all the hard work, and we might go with them hunting.

They left us in care of the squaws and a few old men.

We had no other way by which to get free from this unpleasant situation, but deserting them; for they had been offered one hundred dollars each for four of us, by the citizens of Detroit, but refused it. These four were Major Graves, Samuel Ganoe, John Davenport, and myself.

Thinking this as favourable an opportunity as we could get, I requested Samuel Ganoe to set off with me; he readily consented, and we set off just at dark, and ran to Detroit, which was eight miles, and got to the house of Mr. H., who concealed us in his cellar. He had a hole dug in the bottom of his cellar six or eight feet deep, for the purpose of keeping potatoes; and in this we were put, and he laid planks over it, and threw dirt on the planks, which caused it to bear so nice a semblance to the other part of the cellar, that the Indians could not distinguish it from the common bottom. This dismal dungeon was our abode for half a day, during which time the Indians came, and searched carefully for us, but in vain.

After they were gone, Mr. H. asked a British officer if he would take the care of us. He replied in the affirmative, and then sent us immediately to the fort at Detroit, where we were kept two days, the Indians still searching for us. On the second night about midnight, we were sent to Sandwich, and kept there two days with but little to eat, and then sent to Malden. We found the force at Malden to consist of sixty Canadian French, besides eighty who had received wounds at the River Raisin, and who would no doubt remain invalids for life. We also found stationed at Malden James Girty, who, I was informed, was brother to the infamous Simon Girty; his business was to receive scalps from the Indians; his pay for this service was three dollars per week. I saw here about half a bushel of scalps in a kettle! the number I cannot guess at.

After every exertion to take Fort Meigs had failed, the British returned to Malden, cursing Harrison for a rabbit, which they swore had burrowed, and which they could not take in that situation.

From Malden we were taken across to Cleveland, on the 16th day of May, 1813.

The following prisoners were with the Indians at the time I was a prisoner, *viz*: Major Graves, Jarret Dougherty, Thomas Jones, Joseph Foddre, and John Fightmaster; the latter of whom had deserted from us, was brought back, and made to ride the wooden horse. He then deserted to the Indians, swearing he had rather stay with them than ride Winchester's *English mare* again.

I heard of three prisoners, but do not remember their names; two of whom were about twenty miles from Detroit, and the other near Malden.

From Cleveland nothing worth relating occurred until I arrived at home, in Bourbon County, Kentucky; where I found my friends all in good health, my father excepted, who had gone to face the same enemy from whom I had just made my escape.

Narrative of Mr. John Davenport

During the battle which was fought on the 18th of January, 1813, between the American forces, under the command of Colonel Lewis, and the combined British and Indians, I received a wound in my right leg by a ball which fractured the bone, but did not entirely break it. After the battle was over I, with many others who were also wounded, was carried off the field arid put in a house, where we remained until after the battle of the 22nd, when we were surrendered prisoners of war to the British. I remained here during the night of the 22nd, with the expectation of being carried to Malden the next day, but in this I was disappointed.

On the morning of the 23rd, I witnessed the most horrid scenes of cruelty imaginable; for the British, instead of sending sleighs, as was most solemnly promised, to convey the wounded prisoners to Malden, sent the Indians, who, after selecting a few from amongst the wounded, tomahawked and scalped the rest in the most savage and cruel manner that malice could invent, or devils incarnate execute, and set fire to the houses in which they had been and burned them to ashes! Then, instead of going to Malden, they took me to Brownstown, where I had nothing to eat except a little parched corn.

While I was at Brownstown an Indian asked me whether I had a squaw, to which I answered in the negative. He then replied, "*We make an Indian of you, and by'n by you have a squaw, by'n by you have a gun and horse and go a-hunting*" The next day we proceeded on our march until we came near the River Rouge, where the Indians procured some provisions, consisting of fresh meat, but no salt. From here we set off again and travelled slowly (I rather think to favour the wounded) until we arrived at their encampment, three or four miles from Detroit, at which place there were a number of squaws and children who had taken up winter quarters.

As soon as we had arrived at this place I was presented to an old squaw, whom the Indians instructed me to call by the appellation of "mother." This old witch, as I took her to be, had lost two sons at the River Raisin; I had therefore to supply the place of one of them, and thus had to become the adopted son of the most hideous of all animals that ever roamed over the forests of North America. After this they dressed my wound for the first time, which now appeared to be getting well fast; in the next place they trimmed my hair off, except a small quantity on the top of my head, and painted me; then adorned me with ear-rings, bracelets, &c. and put a band of silver round my head. By this time I began to look very stylish, or rather made as uncouth and grotesque a figure as any of my *copper-coloured brethren*.

While we remained at this place Mr. Gabriel Godfrey, a citizen of Detroit, offered the Indians one hundred dollars for my ransom, which they refused. I now began to conclude that there were no other means of extricating myself from bondage, unless it were by flight, and therefore determined to embrace the first opportunity that presented.

In a few days after, the Indians presented a squaw to me, who appeared to have little more of humanity than the form, but equally as detestable as my *mother*, although she was younger. This ugly looking creature the Indians told me I should marry! I confess I never was so shocked at the thought of matrimony in my life! I told them "*no good squaw*." They then brought several more of those inhuman-looking creatures, whom I understood were also candidates for conjugal felicity. I told them "*by'n by I have a squaw*." This appeared to satisfy them at the present time; in this manner I frequently had to put them off.

They frequently solicited me to wear a breech-clout, which I always refused. One time my mother discovered me mending my pantaloons; thinking this a good opportunity to get me to wear one, she immediately brought one, which I took hold of and said "no good," then threw it down and stamped on it. At the sight of this she was very much enraged, and scolded desperately to herself in her own Indian dialect. I have often wondered since that they did not kill me for disobeying their orders, for I was extremely obstinate, and scarcely ever complied with their injunctions.

Notwithstanding my disobedience the Indians treated me as well as was in their power, especially my mother, who was very kind to me. Some considerable time I had to eat my victuals without salt. I knew they had none, yet I would always ask for some. My old "mother," after some time, procured some for me, which she kept hid to prevent the others from making use of it, and never failed to give me a small portion when I was eating.

Intoxication is practised by the squaws as well as the men; they frequently have drunken frolics, at which times it is dangerous for prisoners to be amongst them. During these frantic revels the prisoners are kept hid by the squaws (a part of whom keep sober) to keep them from being murdered. One night, after the rest had gone to bed, my "mother," who had stayed out later than usual, came in, sat down, and began to sing; she did not appear to be in her senses; I soon discovered that this old priestess of Bacchus had got very drunk. In this mood she seized hold of the fire and threw it on those who were sleeping round the fire, which soon caused them to rise; she then jumped into the fire and danced until she had burned the soles of her *moccasins* off.

They continued here about a month, and then removed about eight miles on the River Rouge, in order to prepare for making sugar. While we were employed at this business a Frenchman persuaded me to marry a squaw, if they insisted, for I would then be treated with more respect, and consequently would have greater liberties. After mature consideration, I thought probably this would be the best plan I could adopt, in order to make my escape, and therefore resolved to marry the next one that was presented to me. It was not long before they brought me a squaw (the most decent looking one I had seen), whom I resolved to marry without hesitation. I however, when just on the point of forming a connubial alliance with her, was prevented by an Indian, who claimed her as his squaw.

Several weeks before the Battle of Fort Meigs, the Indians began to collect and dance the *war-dance*.

Just before the Indians marched they prepared a number of hoops, both ends of which they stuck in the ground and spread their blankets over them. In this place they put hot stones, threw water on them, and then went in themselves and remained until they were wet with sweat. This I conjectured was done in the way of devotion, or in imploring the assistance of the Great Spirit in their intended expedition.

When the Indians marched I was committed to the care of the squaws and a few old invalids. Thinking this the most favourable opportunity I could get, I was determined to put my plan in execution. At night I lay down with the intention of starting when the moon arose, but overslept my time and did not awake till daylight. I arose and started, notwithstanding I was apprehensive of being discovered, and ran directly to Detroit, a distance of about nine miles, probably in as short a time as any Indian in the nation could have performed the same journey.

As soon as I had arrived at Detroit I went to Mr. T. S's, who had persuaded me to run away, and he and his friends would conceal me, which they did accordingly. It was but a short time before a Frenchman, of the name of Shover, and some squaws, came in search of me, but could not find me.

From here I was sent to Sandwich, and concealed there two days, and suffered extremely for provisions. From Sandwich I was sent to Malden, where I found six of my fellow-prisoners, who, together with myself, were kept under close confinement in the fort for three weeks. While we remained here we frequently heard from the rapids, but the news was always favourable on the British side. One morning an old man, who looked as if he had just emerged from the lower regions, came into the fort and exclaimed, "good news, gentlemen! good news! we have killed *fifteen hundred Yankees*, and have taken Harrison and all the rest that were at the fort prisoners!!" I was informed afterwards that this old man was the notorious Simon Girty, so much renowned for cruelty and slaughter, and who has delighted in the shrieks of dying women and *expiring infants!*

From the most correct information I could obtain, their forces at the siege of Fort Meigs, consisting of British regulars, Canadian militia, and Indians, amounted to five thousand!

From Malden I was taken across to Cleveland, and from there I pursued my journey towards the delightful regions of Kentucky, where I arrived in Montgomery County, in June, 1813.

The Battle of Raisin

On the 22nd of January. 1813.
(Parody on Hohenlinden.)

On Raisin darkness reigned around,
And silent was the tented ground,
Where weary soldiers slept profound,
Far in the wintery wilderness.

No danger did the sentry fear,
No wakeful watch at midnight drear;
But ah! the foe approaches near,
Through forests frowning awfully.

And ere the sun had risen bright,
Fast flashing mid the stormy fight,
The thundering cannon's livid light
Glared on the eye most frightfully.

Then deadly flew the balls of lead!
Then many of the foemen bled,
And thrice their banded legion fled,
Before Kentucky's bravery.

And long our heroes swords prevail:
But hist! that deep and doleful wail—
Ah! freedom's sons begin to fail,
Oppressed by numbers battling.

Rise! rise! ye volunteers, arise!
Behold! your right-hand column flies!
And hark! yon shout which rends the skies!
Where Indians yell tumultuously.

Rush o er the bloody field of fame,
Drive back the savage whence he came!
For glory waits the victor's name,
Returning home exultingly.

'Tis done. The dreadful fight is o er;
Thick clouds of smoke are seen no more—
The snowy plain is red with gore,
Where fell the friends of liberty.

                                    Campbell, (not by)

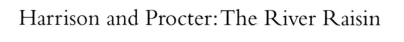

Harrison and Procter: The River Raisin

Contents

Harrison and Procter: The River Raisin   145

The River Raisin

The capture of Mackinac had decided General Hull to abandon the important, but isolated post at Chicago, a measure that had long been contemplated. About the first of August he prepared an order to Captain Heald, the commandant, instructing him to destroy or distribute among the neighbouring Indians all public property that he was unable to remove, to dismantle the fort and join him at Detroit, and sent it to the commanding officer at Fort Wayne to be forwarded by a trusty messenger. At the same time Captain Wm. Wells, the Indian agent at the latter post, was directed to assemble a band of friendly Indians with whom he was to proceed to Chicago and escort the garrison in its retreat. The message to Heald was delivered on August 9th and gave him the first information of the fall of Mackinac.

His intention of evacuating the fort was immediately made known to the Indians who rapidly assembled to the number of several hundreds to receive their presents. They encamped on the sand hills overlooking the lake a mile or two away and their general demeanour was orderly and peaceful. The merchandise in the government store and a quantity of provisions were given to them: but the spirits and all spare arms and ammunition were destroyed, greatly to their disappointment. On the 11th Captain Wells arrived at the head of one hundred mounted Indians. Two days later Heald began his march along the sandy beach in the direction of Detroit, with his Indian escort forming an advance and rear-guard.

His main body was composed of fifty-four officers and men of the 4th United States Infantry, twelve armed civilians, nine women and eighteen children, several of whom also bore arms. A small train of waggons and pack horses conveyed their baggage and provisions. Two small brass cannon were thrown into the river; but no attempt was made to destroy the fort or neighbouring houses through fear of provoking the Indians. When they rushed forward to ransack the deserted buildings they found to their intense disgust that the powder magazine had been emptied into the well and that a large number of firearms had been broken up and barrels of whiskey emptied on the ground. As these were precisely the articles that they most coveted, their indignation knew no bounds.

A numerous party started swiftly in pursuit and after running two or three miles at full speed gained a commanding position on the crest of the sand hills about a hundred yards to the right of the route by which the column must pass. Their actions seemed so menacing to Heald that he rashly ordered his small body of infantry to move against them and expel them at the point of the bayonet. As the Indians showed no disposition to retire the soldiers fired a volley and charged. The Indians gave way in front but closed in upon their flanks and rear, delivering a deliberate and effective fire from the cover of thickets and hollows. In the course of fifteen minutes two-thirds of Heald's men were killed or wounded, his baggage train was captured, and the survivors forced to take refuge upon a mound in the adjacent prairie where they stood desperately at bay.

They were not immediately pursued: but all the wounded men who were left behind and most of the women and children captured with the waggons were mercilessly slaughtered. Captain Wells was among the killed but his band of friendly Indiana abstained from the contest and finally rode out of sight. Heald was badly wounded and the total destruction of his party could have been accomplished with ease. But instead of renewing the attack, the Indians assembled and held a consultation after which they signalled to him to come forward. Heald gallantly advanced alone and was met by Blackbird, a noted Ottawa chief, accompanied by a half-breed interpreter. After shaking hands Blackbird invited him to surrender promising that the prisoners should be well treated. As further resistance was evidently hopeless, Heald agreed to this proposal with little hesitation, although still doubtful of the Indians' sincerity.

Thirty-eight men, of whom twenty-six were regular soldiers, two women and twelve children had already perished. Mrs. Heald and several other persons were suffering from wounds. After being disarmed the prisoners were marched back to the Indian camp where they were apportioned among the different bands. Next day Fort Dearborn was burnt and the Indians dispersed to their respective villages. Heald and his wife were taken to the Ottawa village near the mouth of the River St. Joseph where they were allowed to reside at the house of Benoit, a French Canadian trader. A few days later many of the warriors marched away to besiege Fort Wayne and Heald took advantage of their absence to induce a Canadian to take them in his boat to Mackinac where they were kindly treated by Captain Roberts who supplied their wants and furnished them with a passage in the next vessel sailing for Detroit.[1] The earliest information received by Procter, about the 8th of September, led him to believe that only three persons had escaped death and made him tremble for the fate of the garrison of Fort Wayne, which was described as being closely invested and reduced to the last extremity.

Until that moment he had no intimation that an attack upon Chicago was contemplated nor were the Indians in that quarter considered as coming within the influence of the officers of the British Indian Department.[2] Further inquiry proved that the collision was unpremeditated and that some thirty prisoners were scattered amongst the Indian villages on the borders of Lake Michigan. Chief Justice Woodward then requested that several messengers should be despatched to ransom the survivors and conduct them to Mackinac or Detroit. Procter promptly replied that the most effectual means in his power would be employed at once "for the speedy release from slavery of these unfortunate individuals and for their restoration to their friends."[3] Elliott and McKee were accordingly directed to make known his wishes to the chiefs and readily secured their promise that the captives should be surrendered.[4]

Lieutenant Helm and a few others were soon brought in, but the Indians became greatly angered at the destruction of some of their villages and decided to retain the remainder as hostages for the safety of their own people who had been carried away as prisoners. When Robert Dickson visited Chicago in the following March he ascertained that seventeen soldiers, four women and some children were still prisoners among the neighbouring Indians and took instant measures for their redemption.[5] Eventually most of them were liberated through his influence.

Every available vessel and boat was pressed into service for the

---

1. Heald to Eustis, Oct. 23, 1812; A. B. Woodward to Procter, Oct. 8, 1812.
2. Procter to Brock, Sept. 10, 1812.
3. Procter to Woodward, Oct. 10, 1812.
4. Procter to Evans, Oct. 28, 1812.
5. Dickson to Freer, March 16, 1813.

transportation of the prisoners taken at Detroit: but with every effort, several weeks elapsed before the last of them were sent away. The regular troops were taken to Fort Erie on their way to Quebec and the Ohio volunteers and drafted militia were paroled and landed at Cleveland. The detachment of the 41st Regiment which had been drawn from the Niagara frontier was sent back without delay to meet the impending attack in that quarter and the militia volunteers from the counties of Lincoln, Norfolk and York returned to their homes, after doing duty as an escort to the prisoners on their way down the lake.

Three hundred of the local militia were retained in service, part of whom were employed in the expedition to the River Raisin and Miami Rapids already described, while the remainder were engaged in disarming the Michigan militia, dismantling the batteries at Detroit and removing the guns and military stores to Amherstburg The executive powers of civil governor of Michigan Territory were assumed by Colonel Procter, who appointed as Secretary for the time being, Augustus B. Woodward, the former Chief Justice. All officers of the American Indian Department were superseded and collectors of customs were appointed. All other civil officers remaining at their posts within the conquered territory were continued in office by special proclamation. Persons having public property in their possession were required to deliver it up to the officers of quartermaster-general's department without delay.

On arriving at Fort Erie, Brock learned that an armistice had been concluded and at once wrote to Procter to suspend the projected expedition against Fort Wayne until further orders.[6] Eight hundred Indians took their departure from Amherstburg within a few days in high dissatisfaction in consequence. The Prophet returned to the Wabash and Tecumseh undertook a long journey to the south in the hope of regaining his health and enlisting the Cherokees and Creeks in the war. Early in September, Procter advanced with a small force to the Miami Rapids where he learned that the enemy's post at Sandusky had been abandoned, and that Chicago had been taken and Fort Wayne closely invested by the "back Indians." Colonel Elliott who had accompanied him on this expedition was disabled by illness from riding on horseback or he would have sent him forward to restrain them; but he was instructed to take all necessary measures for that purpose within his power.

6. Brock to Procter, Aug. 25. 1812.

On the 10th of September, after his return from Detroit, he received a letter from Brock informing him of the resumption of hostilities and desiring him to send every man and gun he could spare to his assistance on the line of the Niagara. A party of Indians had come in about the same time bringing a prisoner who had been sent out from Fort Wayne to seek assistance from General Harrison.[7] By his account the garrison was reduced to such an extremity that Procter decided to despatch a small body of regulars and militia to assist in the siege and save the lives of the inmates. Some American prisoners to whom his determination was made known seemed much pleased and gave him full credit for his good intentions.[8]

Fortunately, as it happened, some unforeseen events delayed the departure of this expedition for several days. The regular troops at his disposal had been reduced to less than two hundred and fifty of all ranks and arms by the detachment of parties to serve as marines and escorts and he was consequently obliged to call out a hundred additional militiamen besides thirty horsemen to act as despatch riders and maintain his communication with the settlement on the Thames. One hundred and fifty Indians opportunely arrived from Mackinac, which with the Wyandots and other small bands that still remained at Amherstburg made up a body of about six hundred warriors. The announcement that the war would be continued put them all in the best humour and they seemed eager for active employment. Twenty artillerymen under Lieut. Troughton with a light howitzer and two small field guns, one hundred and fifty of the 41st Regiment and an equal number of the Essex militia and the whole of the Indians were accordingly detailed to march against Fort Wayne.

Brevet Major Muir of the 41st was selected for the command as an officer of tried courage and discretion. Colonel Elliott and Captain Caldwell were placed in charge of the Indians. Forty-seven French Canadians from the River Raisin were engaged to drive a large herd of cattle and a train of pack-horses escorted by the Indians, many of whom were mounted on their own horses, while the artillery and infantry ascended the Miami in boats of tight draught as far as they could go. The distance to be travelled exceeded two hundred miles, much of which would undoubtedly be difficult navigation owing to prolonged dry weather.

These preparations detained Muir until the 16th of September,

7. Letter in Boston Messenger, Dec. 1. 1812. Procter to Brock, Sept. 10, 1812.
8. Brock to Prevost, Sept. 18, 1812.

when he set sail from Amherstburg. The troops were landed at the foot of the rapids, where the tedious labour began of conveying the artillery and stores across a ten mile portage and of towing the boats upstream. Here they were joined by their supply train and a considerable body of Indians. The water in the river was unusually low and after surmounting the rapids their progress was slow and fatiguing. The Indians persistently lagged behind and gave little assistance of any kind. On the afternoon of September 26th, Muir arrived at the old Delaware town twelve miles above the site of Fort Defiance at the junction of the Au Glaize with the Miami and forty miles below Fort Wayne.

Three days had been occupied in moving his boats a distance of only eight miles. The guns were landed and remounted on their carriages with the intention of advancing the remainder of the way by the Indian trail. The main body of the Indians had remained behind at Fort Defiance; but for the first time a few of their scouts had that day been induced to precede the troops a few miles. About sunset this party discovered five white men forming their camp for the night, whom they quietly surrounded and approached, stating that they were hunters on their way home. Ensign Leggett, the officer in command, informed the Indians that his party were scouts for General Winchester's army of five thousand men which had relieved Fort Wayne exactly two weeks before and was then encamped only four miles in their rear, while another body, three thousand strong, was advancing down the Au Glaize with the intention of joining Winchester at Fort Defiance when the whole force would move forward to the rapids.

The Indians then declared themselves as enemies and demanded his surrender. Seeing that he was outnumbered and that resistance was useless Leggett finally consented to accompany them to the British camp on the condition that his men were not disarmed. After proceeding together in that direction until night fell, the Indians became suspicious that their prisoners intended to escape, when they were all ruthlessly shot down and scalped. This took place so near Muir's encampment that the sound of the firing was distinctly heard by the sentries and caused a general alarm.[9] Muir at once sent off a runner with a message to summon the Indians to his support and took up a position on the high ground commanding a ford in the river.

At noon next day Elliott came up with six hundred warriors and scouts were sent out to explore the woods in every direction. At

9. Muir to Procter, Sept. 26, 1812; Richardson (Casselman's ed.), pp. 94-5.

nightfall, Split Log, a Wyandot chief of reputation, reported that he had gone entirely around the enemy's camp which was situated about eight miles away and was strongly fortified. He estimated their force at about 2,500 men.[10] Winchester's advance from Fort Wayne had been conducted with great caution in three parallel columns, a few hundred yards apart, with his supply train in the centre and an advance guard of three hundred men preceded by a screen of scouts thrown out a mile or two in front. Moving at a rate of between five and ten miles a day he invariably halted about three o'clock in the afternoon and surrounded his entire camp with a formidable breastwork of logs and brush. When it became dark large fires were built fifty paces outside his lines and smaller ones at the door of each tent.[11]

On the morning of the 27th much dismay was caused by the discovery of the mutilated bodies of Leggett's party and Winchester at once drew in his flanking columns and retired to his camp which he began to strengthen in expectation of an attack.[12]

Muir was already in difficulties from lack of supplies, many cattle having run away from their drivers. He had in consequence only sufficient provisions for two days' consumption although his whole force had been put upon short allowance several days before. A party had been sent back to the rapids to procure cattle but had not yet returned. Next morning one hundred and fifty more Indians came up, increasing his force to more than a thousand men but at the same time adding to his embarrassment in providing food. Concluding that the approach of so large a force indicated an immediate intention to advance upon Detroit or Amherstburg, Muir sent off a despatch to warn Procter and boldly determined to attack Winchester on his line of march if he gave him an opportunity.

Captain Caldwell and Lieut. Askin went forward to reconnoitre with sixty militia and Indians. They returned after a brisk skirmish in which they lost two men and reported that the enemy's advanced

---

10. Muir to Procter. Sept. 20, 1812; Richardson, p. 95.
Brigade .Major Garrard reported the strength of Winchester's brigade, Oct. 31, 1812, as follows:—
Regiments of Allen, Lewis and Scott fit for duty 1,678, 'Sick' present 216 fit for duty, absent 231, totalling 1,894 fit for duty.
Winchester had also under his command Simrall's dragoons 300 and Garrard's troop of mounted riflemen 70 totalling 380 making a final total of 2,274
11. Letter in Federal Republican of Georgetown, DC, Nov. 27, 1812. dated Paris, Ky., Oct.
12. Tupper to Harrison, Oct. 12, 1812.

party was already within two miles. The guns were placed in a position to command the approaches to the ford and by which the Americans must cross the river, with the regulars and militia in support; but the Indians positively refused to fight at that place and Muir was obliged to retire to his boats. The guns and stores were embarked and sent away in charge of Lieut. Troughton. Muir then went to the Indian camp where a council of the chiefs was assembled to decide upon their future course. He was soon informed that they had determined to fight in the morning at some advantageous spot.

An hour before daylight to his great surprise he received a message from Colonel Elliott stating that their soothsayers had been busy conjuring all night and in consequence the Mackinac and Saginaw Indians were preparing to return home at once. Assuming that he had then no alternative to an immediate retreat, Muir gave orders for his baggage and cattle to be sent off. Shortly afterwards he received a second message from Elliott informing him that the Indians had changed their minds and were determined to fight. On marching his troops to their encampment he found that they were not yet ready to move, but that small parties were going off in every direction. The chief of the Mackinac Indians came to take leave of him saying that as the Indians could not agree among themselves he would take his young men home; but he was willing that those who had horses should remain if they chose, as they could easily escape in case of a defeat. He then went away followed by most of his band. Muir observed to some of the interpreters that the number of Indians that remained seemed very small.

Overhearing this a young Huron exclaimed that there would not be half as many by the time they reached the ground they had selected to fight on, which lay in the fork of the river about three miles above Fort Defiance where both their flanks would be protected by branches of the Miami. The movement was begun and Muir rode forward with Elliott to examine this position. On their return a prisoner was brought in who gave his name as Sergeant McCoy of Scott's regiment of Kentucky volunteers. He had been wandering in the woods for four days without food. On being questioned he described Winchester's force very accurately giving the name and approximate strength of each regiment and estimating the whole to amount to three thousand, of whom four hundred were dragoons or mounted riflemen, accompanied by a six pounder and a train of seventy waggons. They were short of provisions but expected to be joined at Fort Defiance by an equal force advancing down the Au Glaize with provisions for both and four field guns.

By that time Muir had ascertained that not more than 330 Indians had remained and told Elliott that it would be madness to risk an engagement with so small a force, pointing out the danger they ran of being completely surrounded and destroyed by overwhelming numbers. Elliott replied that two of the Indian conjurers had dreamed that they would be successful that day and the warriors were fully determined to fight. Muir bade him tell them that he could not see the smallest prospect of success and must refuse to throw away the lives of his men to no purpose. Roundhead then came to him with an interpreter and urged that they might be allowed at least to justify the prediction of the conjurers by driving back the enemy's advance guard, and then retire through the woods. Muir retorted that the Indians might be able to do this but the regular troops could not exist without supplies.

During the day he overtook Troughton who had been obliged to lighten his boats by the sacrifice of some stores. Indian scouts who were sent up the Au Glaize reported that they had heard cannon shots and the sound of bugles in the woods a few miles up that river, which seemed to confirm the report that an army was advancing from that direction.[13] Muir continued his retreat without molestation arriving at the head of the rapids on September 30th, and at Amherstburg on October 2nd. He reported that his men had behaved remarkably well and praised his officers for "their zeal and cheerful compliance with all orders on every occasion." As it afterwards appeared his movement was not wholly fruitless, as it materially delayed Harrison's advance upon Detroit: but the result of the expedition confirmed Procter in the conviction that he must have "an independent regular force to insure the assistance of the Indians." He strongly urged that he should be reinforced by a portion of the 41st regiment without delay. He wrote:

> The Indians will certainly not desert us now, but a respectable force is requisite to give them confidence and render them effective. The Indians hesitated some time whether they should again confide in us. They have their fears that this territory may be again ceded to the Americans and in the event of which I am confident they will look upon us as their betrayers and worst enemies.[13]

He had already received a letter from Brock approving of his move-

13. Procter to Brock, Sept. 30, 1812.

153

ment against Fort Wayne. He added:

But it must he explicitly understood that you are not to resort to offensive warfare for purposes of conquest. Your operations are to be confined to measures of defence and security. With this view, if you should have credible information of the assembling of bodies of troops to march against you, it may become necessary to destroy the fort at Sandusky and the road that runs through it from Cleveland to the foot of the rapids. The road from the River Raisin to Detroit is perhaps in too bad a state to offer any aid to the approach of an enemy except in the winter, and if a winter campaign should be contemplated against you it is probable that magazines would be formed in Cleveland and its vicinity, of all of which you will of course inform yourself. In carrying on your operations in your quarter it is of primary importance that the confidence and good will of the Indians should be preserved and that whatsoever can tend to produce a contrary effect should be carefully avoided. I therefore most strongly urge and enjoin you acting on these principles on every occasion that may offer, indicating them in all those under your influence and enforcing them by your example, whether in your conduct towards the Indians or what may regard them or in your language in speaking to or of them.[14]

He was advised never to call out the militia except in cases of urgent need and only in such numbers as might be indispensably required. A reinforcement of regular troops was promised when circumstances would permit.

During Muir's absence the *Queen Charlotte* was directed to make a demonstration in his favour by cruising off the south shore of Lake Erie between Cleveland and Sandusky and Procter began to remove the cattle and other supplies from the eastern settlements in the Michigan territory without much ceremony. He announced his intention of leaving no provisions in that quarter for the enemy's subsistence and that he should be made to pay dearly for every inch of tenable ground.[15] He foresaw that a forward movement would not be long delayed since several undesirable persons who had been permitted to leave Detroit might be relied upon to expose the weakness of his force. The governor general had indeed recommended the total evacuation

---

14. Brock to Procter, Sept. 17th.
15. Proctor to Brock, Sept. 30, and Oct. 3, 1812.

of Detroit and the entire territory of Michigan to enable Brock to withdraw a greater number of regular troops to the Niagara frontier, but that capable commander exorcised his discretion to postpone this from motives of both policy and humanity.[16]

He wrote:

> Such a measure would most probably be followed by the total extinction of the population on that side of the river, or the Indians, aware of our weakness, would only think of entering into terms with the enemy. The Indians since the Miami affair in 1793 have been extremely suspicious of our conduct; but the violent wrongs committed by the Americans on their territory have rendered it an act of policy with them to disguise their sentiments. Could they be persuaded that a peace between the belligerents would take place without admitting their claim to an extensive tract of country fraudulently usurped from them and opposing; a frontier to the present unbounded views of the Americans, I am satisfied in my own mind that they would immediately compromise with the enemy. I cannot conceive a connexion so likely to lead to more awful consequences.
>
> If we can maintain ourselves at Niagara and keep the communication to Montreal open, the Americans can only subdue the Indians by craft, which we ought to be prepared to see exerted to the utmost. The enmity of the Indians is now at its height and it will require much management and largo bribes to effect a change in their policy; but the moment they are convinced we either want the means to prosecute the war with spirit or are negotiating a separate peace, they will begin to study in what manner they can effectually deceive us.[17]

When the declaration of war became known in Kentucky it received the hearty approval of the great majority of the people and most of the towns and villages were illuminated on the following night as a sign of general rejoicing. As soon as Congress adjourned, Henry Clay, the Speaker of the House of Representatives and recognised leader of the war-party, hurried home and exerted himself with characteristic energy to promote the organization of a volunteer force to support General Hull in the anticipated conquest of Upper Canada. He daily attended musters of militia and frequently stirred

16. Prevost to Brock, Sept. 14, 1812.
17. Brock to Prevost, Sept. 28, 1812.

public meetings with a torrent of fiery and confident rhetoric. Shortly after his arrival at Lexington he wrote to the Secretary of State that he was actually alarmed by the enthusiasm displayed by the people of his State. Four hundred men had been enlisted for the regular army and the quota of militia detached for six months' service had been more than completed with volunteers. He added:

> Such is the character of our society, however, that I doubt whether many can be engaged for a longer period than six months. For that term any force whatever which our population may afford, can be obtained. Engaged in agricultural pursuits, you are well aware that from about this time when the crop is either secured in the barn or laid by in the field until the commencement of spring, there is leisure for any kind of enterprise.[18]

Two weeks later persistent rumours respecting the precarious situation of Detroit excited grave misgivings he wrote confidentially:

> Should Hull's army be cut off, the effect on the public mind would be, especially in this quarter, in the highest degree injurious. Why did he proceed with so inconsiderable a force, was the general inquiry made of me. I maintained it was sufficient. Should he meet with a disaster, the prediction of those who pronounced his army incompetent to the object will be fulfilled, and the Secretary of War, in whom already there unfortunately exists no sort of confidence, cannot shield Mr. Madison from the odium which will attend such an event.[19]

In public he kept up a brave show of confidence and on the very day of Hull's capitulation he addressed three regiments assembled at Georgetown, serenely predicting the speedy capture of Amherstburg and conquest of Upper Canada.[20]

Some time before this, Harrison, the capable and energetic (governor of the Indian Territory, had been invited by Governor Scott to attend a conference on military affairs at Frankfort and his arrival evoked a great demonstration of warlike enthusiasm. Many leading politicians had assembled there to be present at the inauguration of Isaac Shelby, a veteran soldier of the Revolution, as Scott's successor

---

18. Clay to Monroe, July 29, 1812.
19. Clay to Monroe, .Aug. 12, 1812.
20. Williams, Two Campaigns in 1812.

in office. Brigadier General James Winchester of Tennessee had been designated by the Secretary of War to command the forces then being organised but he had not yet arrived and was by no means popular in Kentucky. Steps were immediately taken to secure his supersession by the "hero of Tippecanoe." At the suggestion of a small caucus of influential politicians, Harrison was accordingly appointed Major-General of the Kentucky militia, thus outranking Winchester. On the day of his appointment. Clay wrote in the highest spirits to solicit the same rank for him in the army of the United States.

> If you will carry your recollections back to the age of the Crusaders and of some of the most distinguished leaders of those expeditions. you will have a picture of the enthusiasm existing in this country for the expedition to Canada and for Harrison as commander.[21]

The leader thus chosen was only forty years of age, active, robust and masterful. He had been governor of Indiana for a dozen years and knew the frontier and its people thoroughly. He was a most persuasive and voluble speaker and an adept in the arts of paining and retaining personal popularity. Throughout his first campaign he wore an ordinary hunting shirt and conversed freely with all ranks. His short but fervid speeches from the top of a stump or tail of a waggon went straight to the hearts of his men and never failed to rou.se them to renewed efforts. The Cabinet at this time seriously contemplated the appointment to this command of James Monroe, the Secretary of State, who was eager to display his military talents; but when their hand was thus forced by the unexpected action of Clay and his friends they could not well refuse their assent.[22]

One regiment had already begun its march for Vincennes, and Harrison wrote a lengthy letter to the Secretary advocating the formation of a chain of blockhouses along the Illinois River from its mouth to Chicago as a barrier against Indian raids and the concentration of five thousand men at Fort Wayne. But while on the road to Cincinnati on August 26th he learned with dismay that both Detroit and Chicago had fallen and that Fort Wayne was closely invested. The military situation was wholly changed. Next day he crossed the Ohio with the 17th United States Infantry, the 1st and 5th Kentucky Volunteers, the 1st Kentucky Riflemen, and a troop of dragoons, making

---

21. Clay to Monroe, Aug. 25, 1812.
22. Colton, *Letters of Henry Clay*.

a force of 2,100 men. Three other regiments of infantry volunteers, five troops of dragoons and five hundred mounted infantry were a few days' march in rear.[23] He described these troops as "the best material for forming an army that the world has produced," but qualified this by the statement "that no equal number of men was ever collected who knew so little of military discipline." Nearly the whole of his men were armed with rifles; but he had no sabres for his cavalry and possessed but a single field-gun. He then requested Shelby to call into service an additional body of mounted riflemen for the protection of Indiana and appealed to Meigs to support him with the entire military strength of Ohio.

He assumed control of all military affairs and put his own column in motion for Fort Wayne. At the ford of St. Mary's River he was overtaken by Johnson's regiment of mounted riflemen from Kentucky and a day later by seven hundred horsemen from Ohio, increasing his force to three thousand, of whom thirteen hundred were mounted. In fact every road intersecting his line of march was thronged with unsolicited volunteers eager to join him. His movement was conducted with characteristic circumspection and vigilance and difficulties of transport delayed him; but Fort Wayne was relieved without firing a shot, on September 12th. Strong; columns of mounted men were then sent out in every direction to destroy all Indian villages within sixty miles.

Harrison himself accompanied one of these which marched to the forks of the Wabash.[24] These villages were all deserted at their approach and few prisoners were taken. The cabins were burnt and the standing corn was cut and piled in heaps to rot. Graves were ransacked and the bones they held scattered wantonly abroad. Little was accomplished by these raids except the infliction of untold misery upon a number of wretched women and children and the consequent exasperation of the warriors who were forced to seek refuge at Amherstburg or Brownstown.

During their absence Simrall's regiment of Kentucky dragoons and a troop of mounted riflemen arrived in charge of a supply train, adding five hundred men and rendering possible a further advance. But on September 18, General Winchester came up and assumed command much to the disgust of many of the Kentuckians with whom Harrison had become a general favourite, while his successor seemed distant and supercilious. Winchester prepared to move forward to the

23. Harrison to Eustis, Aug. 28 and 29, 1812.
24. Harrison to Meigs, Aug. 28, 1812.

Miami Rapids and Harrison returned to Piqua with the intention of attempting a simultaneous advance with all the mounted troops he could assemble by way of St. Joseph's River to the River Raisin.[25]

The infantry regiments of Jennings, Barbee, and Poague, in all about fifteen hundred strong, were directed to move down the Au Glaize in charge of a supply train, clearing the road and building blockhouses to protect the line of communication as they advanced. Winchester wrote confidently to Meigs that he still hoped to winter at Detroit or its immediate vicinity and asked him to push forward two regiments of Ohio Volunteers to join him at the Miami Rapids between the 10th and 11th of October, and a third to keep the road open from Piqua to Fort Defiance.

On September 22, he marched from Fort Wayne with about 2,500 men, but seldom advanced more than five miles in a day. Scouting was performed by a small band of Indians led by a half-breed Shawanese chief known as Captain Logan, said to be a nephew of Tecumseh and a company of white spies under Ruddle, a veteran frontiersman.[26] Apprehending an attack from Muir, Winchester crossed over to the right bank of the Miami at a little known ford and fortified his camp. Messages requesting reinforcements and supplies were sent off to Harrison and Meigs. On September 30, he learned that Muir had retreated and moved forward to the site of Fort Defiance where he again formed an entrenched camp and awaited supplies. Nine days had been occupied in covering a distance of less than fifty miles.

On reaching Piqua, on Sept. 24th, Harrison received a letter from the Secretary of War, dated only seven days before, placing him in supreme command of the Northwestern army which, in addition to all the regular troops in the military district, would include the whole of the volunteers and detached militia from Kentucky and three thousand ordered to join him from Pennsylvania and Virginia, making a total force of more than ten thousand men. A train of artillery was being equipped at Pittsburg. With respect to the vital question of supply he was practically given unlimited authority. The secretary wrote:

> Command such means as may be practicable, exercise your own discretion and act in all cases according to your own judgment.

After having secured the frontier against Indian incursions, he was

25. Harrison to Eustis, Sept. 11 and 18, 1812.
26. Harrison to Meigs, Sept. 22, 1812.

instructed to retake Detroit and advance as far into Upper Canada as he might deem prudent with a view to the permanent conquest of that province.[27] The secretary's next letter confirmed and even extended his authority.

As the difficulty of obtaining supplies, particularly of provisions, through the wilderness, appears to be one of the greatest obstacles you will have to contend with, which difficulty it is well known increases as the season advances, your own judgment will enable you to determine how far it may be practicable to advance and what posts or stations it may be expedient to maintain during the winter. You are already apprised of the solicitude of the government that everything that can be done, shall be done towards recovering the ground lost and extending successful operations into Canada.[28]

The contractor, commissary, and all officers of the quartermaster general's department were made directly subject to his orders to enable him to act with greater freedom and vigour. In three days he had framed a plan of operations by which he hoped to concentrate the greater part of his troops at the Miami Rapids, seventy-two miles from Detroit within a month. Considerations of supply and transport as well as his instructions to protect the frontier settlements, induced him to move in three columns. The right division consisting of 250 cavalry, twenty-eight guns and two brigades of infantry detached from the militia of Pennsylvania and Virginia was to assemble at Wooster, Ohio, and thence advance by way of Upper Sandusky where it would be joined by a brigade of Ohio military increasing its strength to five thousand men.

Twelve hundred Ohio military assembled at Urbana were directed to move by Hull's road, while the remainder of the Kentucky troops would join Winchester at Fort Defiance by the Au Glaize route along which they were already distributed. Upper Sandusky, Fort McArthur on Hull's road, and St. Mary on the Au Glaize, were selected as advanced bases. The purchase of two millions of rations was ordered at once for delivery at these posts, much of which was contracted for within a week as both cattle and grain were abundant in the frontier settlements of Ohio.[29] He was, however, much concerned over the

---

27. Atherton's *Narrative*.
28. Eustis to Harrison, Sept. 17, 1812.
29. Eustis to Harrison, Sept. 23, 1812

pressing need of woollen clothing, watch coats and shoes, which could not be so readily procured.

Meigs, a man of exceptional zeal and energy, made every possible exertion to assist him. So successful were his efforts in assembling and equipping the militia of his State that it was estimated that twelve thousand were already under arms.[30] The Indians of Ohio were collected in concentration camps at Sandusky, Zanesville and Wapakoneta, where blockhouses were built for their protection and they were vigilantly guarded.

Shelby in Kentucky was equally diligent in forwarding supplies and reinforcements. Nor had popular zeal in that State at all abated, Clay wrote, on September 21:

> The capitulation of Detroit has produced no despair. It has on the contrary wakened new enthusiasm and aroused the whole people of this State. Kentucky has at this moment from eight to ten thousand men in the field; it is not practicable to ascertain the precise number. except our quota of the 100,000 militia, the residue is chiefly of a miscellaneous character who have turned out without pay or supplies of any kind coming with their own arms and subsistence. Parties are daily passing to the theatre of action; last night seventy lay on my farm, and they go on from a solitary individual to companies of ten, fifty and one hundred.

All ranks and classes seemed animated by the same warlike spirit. John Allen, the most eminent lawyer in the State next to Clay, .Madison, the State Auditor, and not less than seven Congressmen elect, were already serving under Harrison, two or three of the latter as private soldiers. The course of events, however, would soon demonstrate; that these armed mobs were liable to disperse as rapidly as they assembled.

By October 1, Harrison had succeeded in assembling three thousand men in the vicinity of St. Mary. Half of these were mounted and were formed into a brigade under command of Brigadier General Edward Tupper of Ohio. That day he received an urgent demand from Winchester for reinforcements stating that he had come in contact with the advance of a large British and Indian force, and a letter from Erie reporting that three thousand men had left Amherstburg two weeks before with the design of attacking Fort Wayne. He also learned that

30. Harrison to Eustis, Sept. 27, 1812.

Colonel Jennings had halted on his march halfway down the Au Glaize and fortified his position, greatly alarmed for Winchester's safety he determined to proceed to his support with the whole of Tupper's brigade. Riding rapidly forward with a strong escort he reached Winchester's camp near Fort Defiance on the evening of the 2nd. Continued scarcity of provisions had already caused great discontent. During the night Harrison was aroused from sleep by Colonel Allen and other officers who informed him that their men had resolved to return home and that their remonstrances had been answered with insults.[31]

Next morning Tupper's brigade arrived and Harrison promptly addressed the mutineers assuring them that ample supplies would arrive during the day and that they were the advance guard of an army of ten thousand men. His appointment as commander-in-chief was welcomed by them with evident satisfaction and loyally accepted by Winchester himself. A reconnaissance down the river for several miles satisfied him that no immediate attack need be feared. A site for an intrenchment, which became known as Fort Winchester, was selected on the left bank of the Au Glaize near its confluence with the Miami, and Winchester was instructed to rush forward a force to the deserted settlement at the foot of the rapids, to harvest several hundred acres of corn, which was considered "an object of no little importance to the future movements of the army."

He was put in command of the entire left wing including the three regiments of the Kentucky volunteers and a battalion of Ohio militia employed on the road from St. Mary. Harrison then announced his intention of proceeding at once to Wooster to hasten the advance of the right division.[32] The term of enlistment of Johnson's regiment of mounted riflemen having nearly expired, it was allowed to return with him. The remainder of Tupper's brigade, numbering 960 of all ranks, was detailed for the expedition to the rapids taking with them eight days' provisions which nearly exhausted the entire stock of flour in store.[33]

But a small party of hostile Indians was still lurking in the woods who killed an unwary ranger on the opposite bank of the Miami before the march began. Many of the horses were grazing when this became known, but as soon as they could be caught, there was an immediate stampede in pursuit. Small battles of excited horsemen

---

31. Duncan McArthur to ——— Sept. 1812.
32. Atherton, 9-10; Darnell, *Journal*.
33. Harrison to Winchester. Oct. 4, 1812.

dashed through the ford in spite of their officers' efforts to detain them, and scoured the woods in every direction. When they returned their horses were too exhausted to proceed on the march that day.[34] Logan's Indian scouts after examining the trail reported that the enemy seemed to be in a considerable force and they were sent forward next morning to reconnoitre the river below as far as the little rapids, a distance of fourteen miles They came upon Muir's track and perceived that he had returned in great hurry forcing his carriages over logs and tearing up small trees by the roots.

In their absence, camp rumour had persistently magnified the strength of the enemy and there were symptoms of a panic. Simrall's dragoons had received instructions to return to the frontier settlements to recruit their horses, many of Tupper's men announced their intention of going with then. On October 8th he advanced with the remainder to the Delaware village, twelve miles above the rapids, where he found an abundant supply of sweet corn; but on preparing to continue his march next morning, found that he had only two hundred men. As this number seemed too large for a reconnaissance and too small for an offensive movement he decided to return at once to Urbana by Hull's road, greatly mortified by the conduct of his troops.[35]

The departure of the dragoons reduced Winchester's force to less than 1,800 effectives. They had not drawn full rations for a month. They were sometimes without flour, and generally without salt. Some were barefooted, others without blankets; many had torn their clothing to rags in forcing their way through the woods. None of them was supplied with under garments of any kind. More than two hundred were disabled by sickness. Any further advance before the arrival of supplies seemed decidedly unwise. Winchester therefore contented himself for the present with the construction of a palisaded fortification enclosing about a quarter of an acre of ground with log blockhouses at the angles. Several hours daily were spent in drill. Reconnoitring parties were constantly sent out; but his white scouts seldom ventured to go very far into the woods and little reliance was placed on the reports made by the Indians. A party of men who had strolled off to gather wild plums was surprised and five of them killed. On another occasion a detachment of Garrard's mounted infantry was attacked, losing one man killed and another wounded.[36]

---

34. Atherton. p. 12.
35. Tupper to Harrison, Oct. 12, 1812; Atherton, p. 12.
36. Tupper to Harrison, Oct. 12, 1812.

A report of Winchester's advance had reached Amherstburg on October 4th. An officer of the commissariat was then at the River Raisin engaged in collecting supplies. Procter directed Lieutenant Edward Dewar of the quartermaster general's department, to protect him with a party of militia who went forward in boats. Dewar with Roundhead and fourteen Wyandots rode from Brownstown on the 8th, and learned that a false report of the enemy's movements had been purposely raised by some of the settlers to errant an alarm and give them an opportunity of stealing some of the cattle purchased by the commissary. Next day a Pottowatomie chief arrived with his band from the rapids who stated that he had seen a party of Shawanese scouts in the enemy's service at that place the day before and began a conversation with them across the river, but had been driven away by the appearance of American soldiers coming out of the woods. Some of the settlers at the River Raisin, who were armed and mounted, volunteers to accompany Dewar and the Wyandots on a reconnaisance. Arriving at the place at dark on the 10th they carefully examined the fords and roads before entering the settlement. Five townships had been surveyed at this place and sixty-seven families resided here before the war. But one house remained which was occupied by a French Canadian family named Beaugrand, all the rest having been burnt by the Indians.

Many cattle were running wild in the woods, and there were several large fields of standing corn fully ripe. Sending two trusty scouts along Hull's road. Dewar with Roundhead and two others rode twenty-five miles up the left bank of the river. During the night he encountered a scouting party from a camp of Creeks from Florida who agreed to accompany him to Amherstburg. In the morning he was joined by a war party of Kickapoos carrying the scalp of a horseman whom they had shot within the line of sentries at the American camp. They reported that it was occupied by about eight hundred men who were building blockhouses and were in want of provisions. On his return to the rapids. Dewar found that his men had succeeded in securing only twenty cattle out of ten times that number as they were very wild from having been shot at by the Indians; but it was estimated that eight thousand bushels of corn might be gathered.

The settlements at the River Raisin had suffered greatly from the depredations of the Pottowatomies and Delawares whose villages had been destroyed. They had stolen most of the horses, wantonly killed many cattle and hogs and ravaged the fields. Still he reported that three thousand bushels of grain might be obtained. If suitable encouragement was given he believed that many of the people residing there might be induced to remove to Canada and take part in its defence. He recommended that Colonel Elliott with the whole of the Indians then at Amherstburg, numbering some eight hundred warriors should be sent to the rapids to subsist themselves as the stock of provisions was very low.[37]

The arrival of an express with news of the victory at Queenston raised the spirits of the Indians and they readily consented to occupy the advanced position and sent out parties to the enemy. All of them except the Wyandots had lost their entire crop of corn by American raiding parties and were quite dependent on the commissariat. The corn and cattle at the rapids would be sufficient to maintain them for several weeks during which some portions of these necessary supplies might be secured and brought away. The Indians would have employment, the Americans would be prevented from advancing the consumption of provisions would be lessened and time gained for the removal of the surplus produce of the Michigan Territory. Little inducement for the enemy to continue his movement would then remain. Ten days elapsed before this plan could be carried into effect. By that time only two days' provisions were left in store.

A scouting party returned from the River Huron below Sandusky with a prisoner who stated that the blockhouses there were occupied by five hundred men while as many more were employed in cutting a road forward. This information clearly pointed to a converging movement upon the Miami Rapids. The opportune arrival of a speech from the Six Nations accompanied by a scalp taker, at Queenston greatly animated the Indians and on October 30th, Elliott left Amherstburg with 250 Pottowatomies and Delawares embarked in two gun-boats, a small schooner and a number of *batteaux*, while Roundhead and the Wyandots agreed to ride on from Brownstown and join them at the rapids.[38] Procter complained that the Indian department, upon which so much depended, lacked an efficient head.

Although still capable at times of great exertions, Elliott was more than seventy years of age and in poor health. McKee, next in rank, was brave and influential but had ruined his constitution by habitual intemperance. His regular force was too weak to command respect and repress order among the Indians. Including two companies of the

37. Atherton, p. 10.
38. Dewar to Colonel Macdonnell. Oct. 19, 1812.

Royal Newfoundland Regiment detailed for marine duty it had never exceeded four hundred effectives.[39]

Captain Muir was disabled by illness and there were but six company officers serving with the detachment of the 41st. Firmly convinced that the fate of Upper Canada depended upon the maintenance of his position, Procter earnestly asked for a strong reinforcement. A single regiment, he said, would make him perfectly secure and inspire the Indians with confidence. The armed schooner *Lady Prevost* was instructed to cruise off Sandusky and the River Huron to create an alarm.[40]

Early in November, General Tupper advanced from Urbana to Fort McArthur, where a considerable quantity of supplies had been accumulated, with a strong brigade of Ohio Volunteers and sent Hinkton's company of scouts ahead to reconnoitre by Hull's road. Arriving at the rapids on the afternoon of the 7th, Hinkton found the Indians in possession busily engaged in killing hogs and gathering corn. A white man who was seen in a cornfield stalking a flock of wild turkeys, was stealthily surrounded and taken prisoner before he could give the alarm.[41] He proved to be Interpreter Clark of the British Indian Department. When he was brought to Fort McArthur, Clark was significantly warned that his future treatment would depend on the truth of his statements, and he talked freely. He said that the number of Indians at the rapids, exclusive of women and children, did not exceed 250 and described the weak state of the garrisons of Amherstburg and Detroit. This information decided Tupper to make a dash forward with the object of dispersing the Indians and securing the cattle and corn. The distance was seventy-seven miles which he expected to cover in three days.[42]

Every man who was not afraid of fatigue was ordered to draw five days' rations and he began his march on the 10th at the head of 650 well mounted riflemen, taking with him a light field gun. An express was sent to warn Winchester of the proposed movement and invite his co-operation. Finding that the gun impeded his progress it was left behind at a blockhouse fifteen miles in advance of Fort McArthur. The road was very bad and it was the evening of the 15th before Tup-

---

39. Elliott to Claus, October 28, 1812, Procter to Sheaffe, Oct. 30, 1812.
40. Return of November, 25 1812. Royal Artillery, 30; 41st Regiment, 256 Royal Newfoundland, 117.
41. Procter to Sheaffe, Oct. 30 and Nov. 9. 1812.
42. Howe, *Historical Collections of Ohio.*

per arrived at the ford of the Miami two miles above the settlement. His scouts reported that the Indians were encamped near Beaugrand's house on the opposite side of the river and their boats were moored some distance below. They were drinking and dancing and seemed unaware of his approach. He determined to cross at once, surround their camp in the dark and attack at daybreak. But the river was swollen by recent rains and the current was swift. Very few men succeeded in gaining the opposite bank, several of whom lost their rifles and others had their ammunition spoiled. They were ordered back and the attempt to cross was abandoned.

When daylight returned Tupper marched his force into the clearing opposite their camp. The Indians assembled in considerable numbers and began a fire of musketry across the river while several shots were also discharged from a field gun. The boats got under way downstream. Observing a body of horsemen riding in the direction of the ford with the apparent intention of threatening his line of retreat, Tupper lost no time in moving off. Some mounted Indians under the personal direction of Colonel Elliott, who was recognised by several Americans, and Split Log, the Wyandot chief, conspicuous on a white horse, crossed the river and harassed his rear guard for several miles. Four stragglers were killed and a number wounded. Hearing nothing from Winchester and finding that his provisions were nearly exhausted, Tupper was compelled to retire at full speed to Fort McArthur where his troops arrived on November 20th, half starved and completely exhausted and disheartened.[43]

During the entire month of October, Winchester had remained quietly in his camp on the Au Glaize, drilling his men and waiting for the arrival of a sufficient quantity of supplies to enable him to advance. From time to time his scouts went out but returned with little information. On October 29th, however, they brought in a prisoner, one William Walker, who had lived among the Indians for thirty years and was married to a Wyandot woman. He represented himself as a deserter from the British service but was suspected of being a spy and little confidence was placed in his statements.[44] The lack of proper food and clothing had caused much suffering and discontent. The number of sick had greatly increased and there were several deaths daily.

On November 2nd, Winchester crossed the Miami and advanced a few miles. He fortified his camp in the usual manner and remained

---

43. Tupper to Meigs, Nov. 9th, 1812.
44. Tupper to Harrison. Nov. 19. 1812: McAfee, p. 171; Armstrong. 1, 63-5.

stationary for a week. His scouts then reported the presence of a considerable body of Indians at the rapids. Scarcity of provisions still prevented him from bringing forward the regiments in rear which would have doubled his force, but could be more readily supplied on the line of communication.[45] On November 10th he advanced six miles to a position where there was plenty of timber at hand suitable for the construction of boats or sleds and again entrenched. Next day this movement was reported to Elliott, who became decidedly uneasy as the Wyandots had not yet joined him. and he urged Procter to support him with all the regular troops he could spare and some pieces of artillery.

Tupper's message stating his intention of advancing upon the rapids was not received by Winchester until the 15th, when he at once directed Colonel Lewis to march to his support with 410 picked men. Lewis had advanced eighteen miles when he was overtaken by an express with information that Tupper had arrived at the ford but had failed to cross the river. He then sent an officer with an escort through the woods to propose to Tupper a junction of their forces at Roche de Bout, six miles above the rapids. This party returned next morning with the information that they had found Tupper's camp deserted and the bodies of two of his men scalped and stripped of their clothing. Lewis retreated without delay and on his return Winchester began to strengthen his breastworks and to build huts to shelter his men. Scouts were sent out daily who reported that the Indians continued to occupy their position until the end of November, only withdrawing when the supplies at that place were consumed or removed.

The sole incident worthy of notice occurred on the 22nd, when Logan and two other Shawanese scouts encountered Interpreter Elliott with a small party of British Indians. Finding themselves outnumbered, Logan and his companions professed to have deserted the American service and asked permission to accompany Elliott to his camp. That officer, who was a son of Colonel Elliott, lately practising law at Amherstburg, seems to have been completely deceived and unwisely allowed them to retain their arms after proceeding quietly for some distance they suddenly sprang behind trees and opened fire upon Elliott's party, wounding him and two Indians. Their fire was returned and Logan received a mortal wound but escaped to die in the American camp. Elliott's injuries also proved fatal within a day or two.[46]

---

45. Atherton. p. 98: Darnell. *Journal.*
46. Elliott to Ironside. Nov. 10, 1812; Elliott to St. George, Nov. 11, 1812.

In the latter part of November, the roads were rendered impassable by frequent showers of rain, which, however, were not sufficient to make the Au Glaize navigable for loaded boats The cattle driven forward for beef became so poor for lack of food that they could scarcely stand up to be slaughtered. Typhus fever continued to rage in Winchester's camp, causing many deaths. When the weather turned cold the health of his men improved and they were allowed to hunt; but scarcely a squirrel or other animal could be found in the woods, although game was usually plentiful.

On his return to St. Mary from Fort Winchester, Harrison found himself obliged to detach a battalion of Ohio militia and a regiment of Kentucky mounted riflemen to the relief of Fort Wayne, which was again threatened by the neighbouring Indians influenced by the Shawnee Prophet, who had re-established his camp upon the Tippecanoe River. He learned at the same time that not only Fort Harrison on the Wabash but distant Fort Madison on the Mississippi near St. Louis had been invested. In compliance with his requisition for troops to protect the frontier of Indiana and Illinois, Shelby had issued a proclamation inviting an unlimited number of mounted volunteers to assemble at Louisville on September 18th, bringing their own horses, arms, and provisions for thirty days. Four thousand horsemen responded to the call and were organized into a division of three brigades under General Hopkins.

Fort Harrison was relieved by him on October 10th, and a few days later he began his march across the open prairie with the intention of destroying the Indian villages on the Wabash and Illinois. His guides lost their way and the troops speedily became dispirited and unruly. The tall dry grass caught fire through their own negligence and threatened them with a sudden and dreadful death. The air was filled with thick clouds of smoke that hid the sun. Forage and water for their horses could scarcely be found. Finally the men positively refused to advance further. Their officers confessed that they had lost all control over them and the whole force returned to Fort Harrison where Hopkins organized a smaller column which moved up the Wabash and destroyed the Prophet's town and two other deserted villages, but lost thirteen men in an ambush.[47]

About the same time Colonel Russell and Governor Edwards with a mixed force of rangers and volunteers, among whom were many genuine border ruffians marched from Vincennes against the villages

47. Atherton, 19.

on Peoria Lake which they destroyed without opposition, tarnishing their success by at least one act of almost incredible barbarity. A party of horsemen, commanded by a certain Captain Judy, encountered an Indian and a squaw on the open prairie. The Indian offered to surrender but Judy replied that he had not come out to take prisoners, and shot him through the body. The Indian began chanting his death-song and shot one of the party. The remainder instantly sprang from their saddles and sheltering themselves behind their horses opened fire upon the hapless pair. The man soon fell pierced by many bullets but the woman singularly enough escaped unhurt. Her life was spared although soon afterwards these wretches killed a starving Indian child who fell into their power.[48] They scalped and mutilated the bodies of the slain and ransacked graves in search of plunder. Such acts naturally converted the existing hostility of the Indians into an almost insatiable passion for revenge.

When the British officers attempted to restrain them they indignantly retorted:—

The way they treat our killed and the remains of those that are in their graves to the west make our people mad when they meet the Big Knives. Whenever they get any of our people into their hands they cut them like meat into small pieces.[49]

Another body of seven or eight hundred men composed of the First United States Infantry, a company of rangers, and two regiments of mounted volunteers from Illinois and Missouri assembled at Lower Hill near St. Louis and ascended the Illinois to Peoria Lake, the infantry being transported in flat boats protected by bullet-proof wooden shields. A large band of the Sac Nation was compelled to remove to the Missouri under the supervision of Nicholas Boilvin, an able and zealous agent of the American Government, who had been instrumental in persuading a deputation of chiefs from the western nations to visit Washington during the summer. The French Canadian village at Peoria was burnt and its inhabitants removed to St. Louis under the pretext that they had supplied and assisted the hostile Indians. As usual all cornfields in the vicinity were remorselessly laid waste.[50]

About the middle of October, Harrison established his headquarters at Franklinton as a central position from which he could supervise

48. Davidson, *History of Illinois*.
49. Speech of Blackbird to Claus, July 15, 1813.
50. Howard to Eustis, Oct. 13, 1812. Dickson to Freer. March 16 and 22, 1813.

and direct the simultaneous advance of all his columns. His experience in Wayne's campaign twenty years before, determined him to employ a train of one hundred ox-teams for the transport of the artillery with his right division as they would thrive on forage found in the forest on which horses would inevitably starve. He now considered these guns as indispensable to his future success. If the fall should be very dry he still hoped to reoccupy Detroit before winter set in, but if there was much rain, he must delay his movement until the Miami River and Lake Erie were sufficiently frozen to provide a passage for his troops. Meanwhile, a position at the rapids would enable him to wage a desultory warfare against the Indians near the southern end of Lake Michigan. Learning that General Van Rensselaer was being strongly reinforced by militia from New York and Pennsylvania, he wrote to that officer strongly urging him to make a diversion in his favour.[51]

But a heavy fall of rain, combined with the information that most of the farms at the River Raisin had been broken up and in consequence little food for his animals could be obtained in that part of Michigan, made him far less sanguine as two loads of forage must accompany each load of provisions. Already the contractors had been dilatory in the delivery of supplies. It was believed that one of them would certainly clear a hundred thousand dollars from a single contract with the State of Ohio, and Harrison vehemently asserted that this man would rather see his army starve than permit his profits to be diminished by five hundred dollars, and he denounced one of the sub-contractors as being "as great a scoundrel as the world can produce."[52] In consequence of their delinquency two regiments near Fort Jennings were already subsisting on the commissary's stores.

He finally decided to make Upper Sandusky his principal base of supply and began to organise a train of two thousand oxen and pack-horses for that line of communication. But at the same time he gave orders for the construction of boats and sleds at St. Mary's Fort Jennings, and Fort Winchester, to take advantage of a possible rise of water in the river or an early fall of snow. If absolutely necessary he still affirmed his ability to retake Detroit at any time with a flying column of fifteen hundred or two thousand men without artillery, accompanied only by a few hundred packhorses with flour and a drove of beef cattle.

As soon as the surrender of Detroit had become known to Gov-

---

51. Harrison to Eustis, Oct. 23, 1812.
52. Ibid.

ernor Meigs he had called out two thousand militia for the defence of the north-western frontier of Ohio. As the blockhouse at Lower Sandusky had already been abandoned and destroyed, they were directed to occupy positions at Mansfield and the mouth of the Huron Hiver and erect works of defence. One of their first acts was to make an unprovoked attack upon an Indian village near the former place, which they burnt, after shooting several of its inhabitants. They were employed in building blockhouses and cutting roads through the forest in the direction of Sandusky.

This laborious duty soon became distasteful to many of them. About the middle of September General Beall wrote that he almost despaired of obtaining the quota required from his brigade, and that "the unparalleled number of deserters was truly astonishing."[53] Their working parties were occasionally annoyed by Indians, who cut off a few stragglers and carried away a prisoner to Amherstburg about the end of October, from whom Procter secured some important information. The attempt to build a direct road from Mansfield to the Miami was finally abandoned, as it was found that it would be necessary to lay a causeway of logs for a distance of fifteen miles through a continuous swamp.

After a personal inspection, Harrison determined to concentrate the whole force, which had then diminished to thirteen hundred effectives, at the Huron River, and set them to work on the road along the lake to Lower Sandusky, which was not reoccupied until the middle of November. About the same time the Pennsylvania brigade, accompanied by twenty-eight guns and a baggage train of a hundred waggons, arrived at Mansfield and began to crawl forward at the rate of four or five miles a day to Upper Sandusky, whither the Virginians were also plodding through the mud from Wooster.

At last Harrison was constrained to acknowledge that it would scarcely be possible for him to advance beyond the Miami during the winter, as he considered it indispensable to accumulate at least one million rations there before moving farther. This would be sufficient to maintain an army of ten thousand men for a hundred days. The transportation of such a supply would he a task of immense difficulty. He informed the Secretary of War that the country north of the fortieth degree of latitude was:

... almost a continued swamp to the lake. When the streams

---

53. Beall to Meigs, 13 Sept. 1812.

run favourable to your course, a small strip of better ground is generally found, but in crossing from one river to another the greater part of the way at this season is covered with water. Such is actually the case between the Sandusky and the Miami Rapids, and from the best information I could acquire whilst I was at Huron, the road over it must be causewayed at least half the way.[54]

Major Hardin, who had lately returned from Fort Winchester, reported that the road between Piqua and that place was so bad that a waggon could not haul its own forage. All hope of employing mounted men must inevitably be abandoned.[55] Rain enough had fallen to render the roads almost impassable without making the rivers navigable. At best he could only hope to make use of water carriage for his left column as far as the Miami Rapids. He began to despair of ultimate success until he could obtain command of Lake Erie, or at least dispute its control.

Shelby was urged to prepare the public for delay by concurrence in a proposal to disband all the State troops except a sufficient number to maintain the frontier posts and furnish escorts for supply trains during the winter. But the Secretary of War flatly refused to agree to such a mortifying admission of failure, coming so close on the heels of those upon the Niagara and the frontier of Lower Canada.

Harrison, therefore, showed no relaxation in his efforts to push forward troops and stores by each of his three lines of advance, moving constantly from post to post with unflagging energy.

The unsatisfactory result of General Hopkins's movement laid open his left flank, and before sending his cavalry into winter quarters he determined to anticipate any attempt upon his line of communications by raiding parties of Indians by striking at the villages on the Mississinewa branch of the Wabash. It was alleged that some of their inhabitants had participated in the attack upon Fort Wayne, but the majority had certainly taken no part in the war so far. The gravest accusation that could be made against them was that they had failed to attend the council at Piqua in the latter part of August, after being warned that their absence would be construed as evidence that they had withdrawn from the protection of the United States.

Early in October several of their chiefs had visited Harrison at Franklinton fully prepared to extenuate or deny the charges against

---

54. Harrison to Eustis. McAfee, 167-8. 55. McAfee, 177-8.

them, but when he declared he had positive proof of their guilt, they threw themselves upon the mercy of the government and consented that five of their number should remain in his power as hostages until the decision of the President could be ascertained. A white spy had since reported that the war-party among them had quite gained the ascendant, and Harrison feared that these villages would become a rendezvous and base of operations for hostile warriors seeking an opportunity to intercept his trains on their way from St. Mary to the Miami. If they were laid waste and the corn stored up for the winter destroyed, an enemy would be unable to find any means of subsistence nearer than the Pottowatomie villages at the mouth of St. Joseph's River on Lake Michigan.[56]

He detailed for this expedition Simrall's regiment of Kentucky Dragoons, Ball's squadron of the Second United States Light Dragoons, Elliott's company of the 19th United States Infantry, Alexander's volunteer riflemen and Butler's Pittsburg Volunteers, all of whom were mounted and armed with rifles. Lieut.-Colonel John B. Campbell, of the 19th Infantry, a zealous young officer, was placed in command. Under pretence of returning to Kentucky for the winter this force was moved from Franklinton to Dayton, where all ranks were supplied with fresh horses. They were required to carry twelve days' provisions and a certain amount of forage, and be provided with guides. From Dayton they marched to Greenville, where the final preparations were completed. The ground was hard frozen and covered with snow. The distance yet to be travelled was about eighty miles.

On the evening of the third day, when about twenty miles from their destination, it was determined to march all night and attack the nearest village at daybreak. Their approach was discovered by some mounted Indians, and although they advanced at full speed nearly all the men in the village succeeded in making their escape, leaving about forty women and children behind. In the pursuit several Indians were killed. Three small villages a few miles distant were found entirely deserted. These were at once destroyed, although one of them belonged to the band of a chief named Silver Heels, which Campbell had received special instructions to spare as undoubtedly friendly. Very little corn was found, much to his disappointment, as his horses were already suffering from want of food.

So little resistance had been offered that he had lost only two men killed. But his troops were so greatly fatigued that he determined to

56. Harrison to Secretary of War, 23 Oct., 1812 and Nov. 15, 1812.

fortify a position and encamp for the night. Outlying pickets were posted in small outworks built for their protection. During the night Indians were discovered lurking about, and the camp was placed on the alert two hours before daybreak. While it was yet dark one of the pickets was surprised and driven in with the loss of its commanding officer and several men. This was followed by a general attack on the right flank and rear, during which the assailants directed much of their fire upon the horses, causing indescribable tumult and confusion.

As soon as daylight returned they retired, having so roughly handled Campbell's force in the course of an hour that he abandoned his design of advancing against their principal village about twelve miles farther on and decided to return to Greenville at once. He had lost two officers and six men killed and four officers and forty-four men wounded, besides 107 horses killed and many wounded. His departure was hastened by a false report that the redoubtable Tecumseh, with several hundred warriors, was not far distant. Many men were suffering from frostbites, and there was a danger that their provisions would be exhausted before they could obtain a fresh supply, as their movement must be necessarily slow, on account of the wounded and many dismounted men.

An officer was accordingly despatched in haste to request that a reinforcement with supplies should be sent forward to meet them. During the retreat, whenever they encamped they surrounded their position with a strong breastwork, and one-third of the entire force was placed on guard. Several of the wounded died of exposure, and when at length they arrived at Greenville, fully three hundred men were found to be disabled from further duty. Of Gerrard's company, which had marched out with seventy-two effectives, only seven remained fit for service on the last day of December. Simrall's regiment was so much reduced that it was at once disbanded.

The expedition had resulted in the destruction of Harrison's cavalry without inflicting any serious loss upon the Indians. He was so greatly disappointed that he undertook a special journey from Lower Sandusky to Chillicothe for the purpose of proposing to Meigs to despatch a body of Ohio troops to destroy the remaining villages. When this plan was rejected, he advised Winchester to abandon his intention of advancing to the rapids and fall back to Fort Jennings.[57] He attempted to conceal his failure by the publication of a general order announcing that Campbell's operations had been attended with

57. Armstrong I, 65–8: McAfee, 177–82: Atherton. 28–9.

complete success.

Yet the paralysing effect of the mud had so greatly discouraged him that he broadly hinted to the Secretary of War that it might be expedient to defer any further advance until a sufficient naval force could be created to protect the movement of his supplies by the lake. This might be done he said, with ac comparatively small expenditure of money. He had nominally ten thousand men under his command: but of these more than six thousand three hundred were reported fit for duty. With the must heroic efforts he had not succeeded in pushing the heads of his columns beyond Lower Sandusky, Fort Necessity and Fort Winchester. His artillery had arrived at Upper Sandusky on December 10th: but the teams drawing it, which had started in the best condition, were quite worn out. He was appalled at the loss of horses, valued at half a million dollars.

Two trips from Fort McArthur to Winchester's camp absolutely destroyed a brigade of pack-horses. The road had become a continuous morass, in which the horses sank to their knees and the waggons to the hubs of their wheels. The drivers were generally the dregs of the frontier settlements, who took little care of either horses or goods. The teams were valued so high that the owners were willing to sacrifice them to obtain compensation. Many waggons were abandoned and their contents lost. No bills of lading were used, nor accounts kept with the teamsters. The loss of public stores was enormous.[58] Nothing could be more disheartening than the "imbecility and inexperience of public agents and the villainy of the contractors" upon whom his army was obliged to rely for their subsistence.[59] Every attempt to make use of the St. Mary and Au Glaize Rivers for the conveyance of supplies had failed.

Dr. Eustis, the Secretary of War, had been forced to resign by popular clamour. Monroe, the Secretary of State, undertook to administer the affairs of that department until his successor was appointed. One of his first acts was to require Harrison:

> To form a clear and distinct plan as to the objects you may deem attainable, and the force necessary for the purpose, and that you communicate the same with precision to this department.

He was cautioned at the same time not to promise the inhabitants

58. McAfee, 183-4: Gardinier Examiner.
59. Harrison to Secretary of War, 12 Dec, 1812.

of Canada anything beyond protection for their lives and property, and advised not to occupy any position which he would be unable to retain permanently.

Before he received this letter, Harrison had actually written to suggest the postponement of further military operations until April and May, by which time a respectable naval force might be created upon Lake Erie. Detroit, he said, would not be tenable unless Amherstburg was also taken. Otherwise he would be compelled to hide his army in the swamps to keep it out of range of the British artillery. Even if both these places were captured his adversary might still retain Mackinac and St. Joseph's Island as long as the Ottawa route remained open, and thus supply the Indians in that quarter. While ships were being built, he proposed to occupy a position at the Miami Rapids with fifteen hundred men, maintain a thousand more in other advanced posts, and accumulate supplies. Contrary to his wishes, Winchester had kept the bulk of his division far advanced and thus immensely increased the difficulty of supplying it.

But on December 18th the prospect on the right seemed so encouraging that he wrote from Upper Sandusky to Winchester instructing him to advance to the Miami Rapids and build huts, to give the impression that he intended to winter there, and prepare a large number of sleds for a future forward movement, but giving his troops to understand that they were to be used for bringing forward supplies from the rear. A week later the miscarriage of Campbell's expedition caused him to countermand this order.

The tone of Monroe's letter obviously irritated Harrison, and he wrote a lengthy and vigorous justification of his conduct. As his former letters had contained frequent allusion to the "monstrous expenditure" incident to military operations at that season, he had construed the silence of the late Secretary of War as an intimation that cost was to be disregarded in his efforts to recover the lost territory. A thousand pack-horses were employed in supplying his right column alone. When a barrel of flour was delivered at the advanced posts it had cost the government $120.[60] A brigade of Ohio troops had been employed in road making; beyond Sandusky for a month. The brigades from Pennsylvania and Virginia were close behind.

The concentration of 4,500 or 5,000 men at the Miami within two or three weeks seemed reasonably certain. A "choice detachment" from these could then be selected for a demonstration against Detroit

---

60. *Boston Gazette*, 8th March, 1813.

and an actual attack upon Amherstburg by crossing the river on the ice. He prudently based his estimate of the force necessary for this enterprise not upon the present strength of the British garrison, which was reported to be almost incredibly small, as most of the Indians had dispersed to their villages, but upon the numbers that might be assembled from other quarters in time to oppose him.

He knew that troops could be brought forward quickly from the Niagara frontier by the "back route" along the Thames, and he might encounter the same regulars who had fought at Queenston three months before, while he said that a mere whistle would be sufficient to recall the Indian warriors. If his force was weak, "the timid, cautious and wavering among the Canadians and Indians" would be encouraged to take the field against him, and if he was unable to carry sufficient supplies with him, he would be compelled to make strong detachments to escort his trains. His former experience of Indian warfare had taught him that it would be unsafe to send a detachment either to the front or rear which was not strong enough to repel the enemy's whole force.

One third of his troops had already become ineffective from exposure and disease. A fine body of recruits from Ohio and Kentucky, composing the 17th and 19th regiments of United States Infantry had been nearly destroyed through want of proper clothing. A suspension of hostilities might become inevitable and he reminded the secretary that General Wayne after an entire summer spent in preparation, had been unable to advance more than seventy miles from the Ohio River, when he went into winter quarters, by Washington's advice.[61]

Having put his right wing in motion, he had returned to Franklinton with the intention of urging forward the centre column, which seemed inert and demoralised since Tupper's return from the Miami. Lack of direct lateral communications seriously imperilled the success of his arrangements.

On December 20 the weather turned so cold that the Miami was frozen, thus putting an end to Winchester's expectations of being able to advance by water. Since the 10th he had been entirely without flour, and his men had been subsisting upon lean beef, fresh pork and hickory roots. His supply of salt had long since been exhausted. Many men were suffering acutely from want of shoes and winter clothing. Probably one hundred had died from disease, and the sight of the

---

61. Harrison to the Secretary of War, 4th and 8th January, 1813. McAfee, 192-9; Dawson, 342.

sufferings of between three and four hundred sick made the camp "a loathsome place."[62] His effective force had been thus reduced to less than sixteen hundred of all ranks. Two days later a good supply of flour, salt, and woollen clothing arrived. With undaunted resolution Winchester began building sleds and ordered forward the effective men of Jennings' regiment from the posts in rear to enable him to resume his advance. While thus employed he received Harrison's letter of the 18th, which had been brought through the woods from Sandusky by an officer conducted by Indian guides. In a week each company was provided with three sleds which might be drawn by one horse or three men.

On December 29, one regiment was sent forward six miles, followed next day by the remainder of the effective men in camp. A despatch was sent to Harrison by the roundabout route of Hull's road, which, owing to stormy weather, did not reach him at Upper Sandusky until January 11th. As some of his sleds were drawn by hand, Winchester's progress was slow, seldom exceeding six miles in a day, and a rapid thaw set in, during which most of the snow went away. On January 2 this was succeeded by a heavy fall of snow, which continued for two days and nights. He was then overtaken by Harrison's message countermanding his movement, which he determined to disregard.

On January 4 the march was resumed, but, the snow being nearly two feet deep, horses and men rapidly gave out, and he did not reach the deserted settlement at the foot of the rapids until the 10th.[63] Here he fortified a position with a timber breastwork on the left bank of the river, where Hull's road crossed it, and began building huts and store-houses. Again a message was sent to Harrison by way of Fort McArthur, which did not reach Upper Sandusky until he had left that place. The messenger followed him to Lower Sandusky, and ultimately delivered the letter to him at the place he had started from.[64]

The term of enlistment of the Kentucky Volunteers would expire in February, and Harrison had requested Winchester to recruit at least a regiment from among them to serve six months longer, stating his opinion that it would be unwise to employ them in any offensive movement unless he succeeded. He soon ascertained that the hardships and privations of the campaign had so greatly dispirited the majority that little could be expected, and replied accordingly.

---

62. Darnell, Journal; Atherton; McAfee. 183-4.
63. McAfee. 200-2; Atherton; Darnell.
64. McAfee. 202-3.

Camp equipage and supplies of all kinds were brought up as rapidly as possible, and a large drove of hogs ordered forward from Fort Jennings. A quantity of corn was discovered in the fields, which Winchester ordered his men to gather and use to spare his flour.

On January 11. a scouting party fell in with a few Indians, whom they pursued, and a skirmish followed in which there was some loss on either side. On the evening of the 13th. two French Canadians from the River Raisin came in with a letter from a spy named Day, who had been sent forward to that place. He wrote that a party of Indians had passed through with the information of Winchester's arrival at the Miami and had threatened to return in force and burn the village. The British were preparing to remove all the cattle and provisions of every kind, and suspected persons were being arrested and confined.

A supply of woollen underclothing had opportunely arrived from Kentucky, which made the men comfortable, and they began to regain their spirits, although the weather had again grown very cold. On January 14th, a second messenger arrived from the River Raisin soliciting protection. Winchester wrote to General Perkins, who was in command at Lower Sandusky, stating that he meditated an advance and asking him to send forward a battalion to his support. On January 15, another French Canadian came with information that two companies of Canadian militia and a body of Indians had arrived at the River Raisin shortly before his departure and announced their intention of removing all the cattle and grain and possibly destroying the village.

An Indian scout afterwards brought in a letter from Day, who wrote from Otter Creek, stating that the British force at Frenchtown consisted of forty or fifty militia and perhaps a hundred Indians, who had positive instructions to remove all the inhabitants to Amherstburg with their horses, cattle, carioles, sleds, grain and provisions of all kinds. An immediate advance might secure three thousand barrels of flour and much grain.[65]

Winchester called a council of his principle officers and asked their advice. Colonel Allen at once took the lead and warmly advocated a forward movement in a speech of such force that it carried the other members with him. As they were unanimously in favour of an advance, Winchester concurred cheerfully and ordered Colonel Lewis, as the next senior officer to himself, to march next morning at the head of ten companies completed to fifty-five men each.

65. Winchester Narrative; Armstrong I, 66-7; McAfee,. 204; Brown.

He had less than fifteen hundred effective men, all Kentuckians belonging to the 17th United States Infantry: 1st Kentucky, Colonel Scott; the 2nd Kentucky, Colonel Jennings; the 5th Kentucky, Colonel Lewis; and the 1st Kentucky Rifles. Colonel Allen. Most of them were strong, hardy, adventurous young men. accustomed to the use of the rifle from boyhood. In the river towns of the Mississippi a Kentuckian was dreaded far more than an Indian, and the name "Kentuck" had much the same significance as "cowboy" in later years. They were thoroughly fearless, reckless, lawless fellows, ever ready to quarrel and fight, who boastfully described themselves as "half horse and half alligator, tipped with snapping turtle."

Quiet folk were shocked by their drinking bouts, frequently ending in duels or savage fights attended by biting and gouging. Horse racing and rifle shooting were their chief amusements. Twenty years before the legislature had passed an act making it compulsory on every white male over sixteen years of age to kill a certain number of crows and squirrels every year. Sometimes as many as two thousand squirrels were slaughtered in a single *battue*, all with the rifle. Auction sales or raffles were scarcely known. When a man announced his intention of disposing of his household goods, his neighbours turned out gun in hand. A mark was set up a price was placed upon an article of furniture, each man paid his entrance money, and the shooting began.[66]

These men had been in service since August 16. They had endured much privation with admirable tenacity and acquired a considerable degree of discipline. Their term of enlistment would expire in a month and they were naturally eager to perform some noble action before returning home. Allen had declared that if they failed to advance now, they would be told that "a thousand freemen are unequal to a contest with three hundred savages and slaves."[67]

Lewis began his march early on the 17th, taking with him three days' provisions hauled on sleds. A few hours later Winchester received news which induced him to despatch Colonel Allen with two more companies of fifty-five men each to reinforce him, Lewis advanced twenty miles that day, crossing the bay on the ice to a little settlement on Presqu'Isle. The inhabitants came to meet him with a white flag stating that the British had retired from Brownstown. Three hours after dark Allen overtook him. During the night a messenger came from

66. McMaster, *History of the American People* II, 575; Marshall. *History of Kentucky*; Ramsey, *Hist. South Carolina*.
67. Armstrong I. 68.

Frenchtown with information that the number of Indians there was increasing and that Elliot was expected to march from Amherstburg next morning with many more. Lewis transmitted this to Winchester with a request for further reinforcements, but resumed his march shortly after daybreak in the hope of forestalling Elliot's arrival. He divided his force into four battalions of three companies each, under Colonel Allen, Majors Graves and Madison and Captain Ballard, that commanded by the latter being detailed as an advanced guard.

Winchester had remained so long inactive that he had lulled Procter into the belief that he had gone into winter quarters. Tecumseh who was in poor health, had gone southward to rouse the Creeks and Cherokees, The Prophet had returned to the Wabash. The Indians from Saginaw, Mackinac and the borders of Lake Michigan had long since been dismissed to save provisions. The movement of a strong body of Americans up the Illinois in shot-proof boats, with the intention of building a fort near Peoria and ultimately reoccupying Chicago, had been reported. He surmised that their object was to cut off his communication with the most formidable Indians of the west by the establishment of a chain of posts. The chief Mapock, who had been active in the operations against Hull, had assembled a force to oppose them. Repeated applications from the Indians for detachments of regular troops to accompany them on expeditions had been evaded by Procter with considerable difficulty; but when they proposed the organisation of a body of rangers for that particular purpose, he readily gave his approval.

He wrote:

A corps of that description would be, I am convinced, of the highest utility, both in restraining and directing the hostility of the Indians to the proper objects of it.

It might also prove an efficient substitute for the militia, which had few good officers. He proposed the enlistment at first of a single company as an experiment, and recommended that it should be placed under Colonel William Caldwell, who possessed great influence among the Indians and had commanded a company of Butler's Rangers at the Blue Licks and Sandusky thirty years before.

With the exception of the Wyandots of the River Canard and Brownstown and some Pottowatomies and Miamis, who had been driven in by the destruction of their villages, few Indians remained in the vicinity of Amherstburg.

Procter had directed the construction of two gunboats at Chatham and laid the keel of a ship at the Amherstburg dockyard to ensure his supremacy on Lake Erie. Two blockhouses were also projected at important points. But he lacked carpenters and artificers, as well as officers and seamen to man these vessels when they were launched.

On January 13, a party of Indians came in who reported that the enemy had advanced to the foot of the Miami Rapids with a thousand men. Two days before they had encountered their scouts, of whom they had killed two and wounded several, bringing off three captured horses. Procter promptly issued orders for calling out the militia and assembling the Indians. If it became necessary to dislodge the enemy he foresaw that he must employ the whole force.[68]

Two flank companies of the Essex militia, under Major Ebenezer Reynolds, accompanied by a hand of Pottowatomies, were dispatched next day to break up the settlement at the River Raisin and remove the inhabitants. To enable him to maintain his position until this could be effected, he took with him a three-pounder mounted on a sled, in charge of Bombardier Kitson, of the Royal Artillery. Not unnaturally these people were very reluctant to leave their homes and sacrifice much of their property, and they bitterly resented the insolent conduct of the Indians, who killed or drove off their cattle with scant ceremony. As the Pottowatomies were constantly going and coming, their numbers fluctuated greatly, sometime rising above a hundred and sometimes falling as low as twenty.

About noon on January 18, Reynolds learned that a large body of men had been seen approaching along the lake a few miles distant, and made every effort to collect the Indians. The river was solidly frozen and presented no obstacle to an attack from the southward. Three hours later the enemy appeared in force in the skirt of the woods and deployed into three lines in extended order on a very wide front before crossing the cleared ground, with the evident intention of enveloping his position. The field gun was brought into action, but after firing three rounds with no apparent result, it was seen that a party was crossing the river with the object of cutting off his retreat by the road. Reynolds then gave orders for the removal of the gun and retired from the village, which was occupied by the Americans with the loss of only three men wounded.

Some of the inhabitants instantly armed themselves and began firing upon the retreating Indians. The pursuit was continued, with loud

68. Procter to Sheaffe, 13 January, 1813

shouts, across a ravine and through an orchard and some cleared fields into the woods, which were obstructed with much undergrowth, furnishing excellent cover. Kitson made his escape by the road under cover of the fire of an escort of Indians, On entering the woods the foremost pursuers were soon checked, with material loss. Their eagerness and haste exposed them to the fire of unseen foes, who instantly retired and took up a fresh position, where they reloaded and again awaited their approach until close upon them, when they delivered their fire and retired again.[69] The action continued in this way until dark, when Lewis assembled his men and retired to the village, he found that he had lost twelve killed and forty-five wounded, among the latter being three captains. He acknowledged that he had made a serious mistake in allowing his troops to enter the woods at all.[70]

During the night Reynolds fell back to Brownstown. He reported the loss of one militiaman and three Indians killed, but did not state the number of wounded and missing. The Kentuckians asserted that they had taken twelve scalps besides one Indian and two militia prisoners. The Indians accused them of barbarously hacking to pieces one of their wounded warriors with their knives and tomahawks and of cutting strips of skin from the bodies of the slain to use as razor strops.[71]

Lewis sent off a despatch rider to announce his success and ask for a reinforcement to maintain his position, who travelled with such speed that he reached Winchester's camp before morning. On the 17th Winchester had written to Harrison stating that he was sending forward a force to Frenchtown to secure the flour and grain at that place and desiring support in this movement from the light wing of his army. This letter was despatched to Lower Sandusky. He now wrote again, relating the success of his movement and declaring his intention of going forward in person to maintain this advanced position. After instructing Colonel Wells to follow with six companies, numbering almost 330 of all ranks, and leaving General Payne in charge of the camp with about three hundred of the least effective men, Winchester rode forward with his staff and arrived at the River Raisin on the night of January 20.

---

69. Atherton. 39-40.

70. Lewis to Winchester, 20 January, 1813; Procter to Sheaffe; Armstrong; Atherton, 39-40; Darnell; McAfee.

71. John Strachan, Letter to Thomas Jefferson; Blackbird to Claus, July 15, 1813. Palmer, *Travels*.

Harrison at Upper Sandusky had not received Winchester's letter of December 30th until January 11th, when he ordered a forward large drove of hogs and held his train of artillery in readiness to march. On the 16th he received a letter from General Perkins, written the day before, enclosing Winchester's letter to him asking a reinforcement of a battalion. The artillery was at once ordered forward by way of the Portage River, with an escort of three hundred infantry, as this road was sixteen miles shorter than that leading through Lower Sandusky. Supply trains were directed to follow by the same route. Harrison himself went next day to Lower Sandusky, riding so hard that the horse of his *aide* fell dead on their arrival there at nightfall. He learned that Cotgrove's battalion, with a field gun, was under orders to march next morning.

The distance to Winchester's camp on the Miami was only thirty-six miles, but the roads were much blocked by snowdrifts. At four o'clock on the morning of the 19th Harrison received Winchester's letter of the 17th. There were still three battalions of Ohio Militia at Sandusky. Two of which were at once ordered to advance by forced marches to the Miami. Harrison and Perkins drove off in a sleigh to overtake Cotgrove. Finding that their progress was very slow, Harrison mounted his servant's horse and rode on alone. Darkness coming on his horse became nearly mired in a swamp, where the ice gave way under him and he was obliged to dismount and make his way onward on foot. Cotgrove was then ordered to march directly on the River Raisin by crossing Miami Bay on the ice. After a few hours' sleep, Harrison pushed on to the Miami Rapids, where he arrived early on the morning of the 20th. Captain Hart, Inspector-General of the district, was sent forward to inform General Winchester of the movement of troops in his rear and instruct him to hold his position at all hazards. Next day he received a letter from Winchester in which that officer said

> Advices from Brownstown and Malden all agree that the enemy is preparing to retake this place. If he effects his purpose he will pay dearly for it.

A small reinforcement would make him perfectly secure, he added. The two Ohio battalions from Lower Sandusky arrived that night, and General Payne was directed to march at daybreak with the remainder of the Kentuckians to join Winchester. In no respect could Harrison be justly suspected of any slackness in his efforts to support his lieutenant, whom he had constantly treated more as an associate than as an inferior.

Winchester moved so rapidly that he arrived at the River Raisin on the night of the 20th and Colonel Wells came up next day with his detachment, bringing tents and other camp equipage. There was little regularity in their encampment. Lewis had allowed his men to select quarters and settle down wherever they pleased. They were greatly elated by their success and seemed to forget that they had an enemy in the world.[72] Quantities of hard cider had been discovered and some men were drunk and quarrelsome. Desiring to escape the tumult created by "this parcel of dirty, noisy freemen," the general took up his quarters at the house of Peter Navarre on the right bank of the river less than three hundred yards in rear.

He afterwards stated that had he not been encumbered by so many wounded men. he would have retired to the Miami, but there is nothing in his conduct or correspondence at the time to give colour to this assertion. Wells was instructed to encamp his men on the right of the village and then to select a position to be fortified and occupied by the whole force. This was done: but as some of the troops were tired and all of them excited and unruly, no attempt was made to entrench that day.

Patrols were sent out in several directions. One of these reported that they had gone as far as Brownstown without seeing any sign of an enemy. Another had seen two men, whom they suspected to be British officers ride away from a house two miles up the river. All accounts agreed that the number of regular troops at Amherstburg and Detroit was small, and that there was little danger of an attack. Captain Hart, a brother-in-law of Henry Clay, came in with the information that Harrison had established his headquarters at the camp on the Miami the day before, and that a strong reinforcement was on the march. This was publicly announced and put everybody in high spirits. Colonel Wells was sent back to hasten the movement of supplies; but in a letter to Harrison entrusted to him Winchester expressed no anxiety. Late at night a French Canadian arrived with information that a body of British and Indians three thousand strong was assembling at Browns town. This report seemed so absurd that it was generally disbelieved by the principal officers, who were regaling "themselves with whiskey and loaf sugar."[73]

---

72. Atherton, 40.

73. Darnell, *Journal.*

Frenchtown was a compactly built village of twenty dwellings. Besides barns and outhouses, situated on the left bank of the river and on the right of the road leading to Brownstown, surrounded on three sides by a stout palisade of round logs split in halves and set in the ground, rising to a height of eight feet and sharpened to a point at the top. Blockhouses had been built at the angles during the summer and the place put in a position to resist an attack, but Brush had partially destroyed these works before evacuating it in August.[74] The river front was entirely open. All of the buildings were constructed of hewn logs with shingle roofs, and some were clapboarded. With their gardens and orchards they covered a quadrangular space of two hundred by three hundred yards, the longest side being parallel to the river.

Lewis's original command had taken up their quarters in these buildings, where they were comfortably housed. The troops brought forward by Colonel Wells, consisting mainly of men of the 17th United States Infantry and the 1st Kentucky Rifle Regiment, occupied the post of honour on the right, outside the enclosure, some being billeted in detached houses and the remainder encamped in tents. Along the river on both sides for several miles there were farmhouses, forming in the whole a settlement which had a population of more than twelve hundred persons before the war began. North of the village, at a distance of about one hundred yards, a deep hollow ran parallel to the river, crossing the road to Brownstown nearly at right angles, which, with an isolated farmhouse and orchard, afforded some cover to a force attacking from that direction.

Winchester had with him then three companies of the 17th United States, three companies of the 1st Kentucky militia (Scott's regiment), one company of the 2nd Kentucky militia (Jennings), five companies of the 5th Kentucky militia (Lewis), and six companies of the 1st Kentucky Rifles (Allen), making in all a force of about 975 of all ranks, including the wounded and their medical attendants. Orders had been given to strengthen the position, but little had been done beyond cutting some loopholes in the palisades. A general feeling of security prevailed. As the weather was bitterly cold and the snow lay deep everywhere, no outlying pickets were posted and no patrols were sent out during the night.[75]

Procter learned that Reynolds had been driven from Frenchtown at two o'clock on the morning of the 19th. He quickly decided that

74. Williams, *Two Western Campaigns*.
75. Winchester's Statement: A. B. Woodward to James Monroe, 31 January, 1813.

there was no time to be lost in attacking the enemy at that place "with all and every description of force" within his reach. Fortunately most of the young men of the Petite Côte, were celebrating Queen Charlotte's birthday at a public hall where they were warned for service in a body. Captain James Askin's company of the 2nd Essex was detailed as the garrison of Detroit, under Major Muir, who was still enfeebled by illness. A corporal's party of the Royal Artillery and the invalids of other regular corps with the least effective men of the militia were assigned for the occupation of the fort at Amherstburg, under Lieut.-Colonel J. B. Baby. Every man considered fit for field service was marched across the river on the ice to Brownstown, where the Indians were likewise directed to assemble.

By great exertions a force of 578 of all ranks belonging to ten different corps was scraped together. Of these, 366 were regular soldiers or Provincial seamen. Three three-pounders and three small howitzers, mounted on sleds, were manned by squads of the Royal Artillery and seamen and escorted by a company of the Royal Newfoundland Regiment. Four weak companies of the 41st Regiment officered by four subalterns and eight sergeants. formed the backbone of this motley array under command of Captain Joseph Tallon. As inspecting field officer, Lieut.-Colonel St. George superintended the movements of the militia, of whom there were eight small companies commanded by Major Reynolds.[76]

There were nearly five hundred Indians, mainly Wyandots and Pottowatomies, directed by nineteen white officers headed by Elliott and Caldwell. A good number of these Indians were armed with muskets and mounted on their own horses. Before dark, Procter advanced twelve miles to Swan Creek. where he bivouacked in the open air. Two hours before dawn the march was resumed, and just as day was breaking; the head of the column arrived within gunshot of the village. As the deployment began in the fields on the left of the road the drums in the American camp were heard beating the reveille. Then three shots were fired by their sentries in rapid succession, one of which struck down a leading grenadier of the 41st. Procter has been strongly censured for not charging at once with his infantry, instead of waiting for his artillery, which actually made little impression upon the enemy's defences and gave them time to recover from their surprise. But their

---

76. Staff. 3; Royal Artillery, 23; 10th Battalion Royal Veterans, 4: 41st Regiment, 244; Royal Newfoundland, 61; .Marine Department, 28; 1st Essex .Militia, 116; 2nd Essex Militia, 96; Commissariat, 1. Field Train, 1; Royal Engineers, 1.

position was not yet precisely ascertained, and it was still so dark that the palisades with little jets of flame darting from the loop-holes were at first mistaken for a line of men drawn up in front.[77]

Three guns were placed in position in the orchard near the hollow; the others were moved to the right of the road to enfilade the village from that direction, and were supported by a small party of Indians. The whole of the militia and the great body of Indians made a wide circuit to the left to turn that flank. In this they entirely succeeded, and rushing suddenly from their concealment, with shrill whoops upon the 17th United States Infantry, which was wholly unprotected by any breastwork, the men of the corps were seized with a panic and began to retire in much disorder. Winchester came up and attempted to rally them behind a fence. Two companies of riflemen sallied from the village to their support, but were soon borne away in the general flight.

Lewis and Allen joined Winchester and endeavoured to form the fugitives under the shelter of the river bank, calling upon them to incline to the centre and seek refuge in the enclosure. But the pursuit was keen, and their words were unheeded. The flight was continued across the river and through a narrow farm lane leading past Navarre's house to the main road. Many fell beneath a murderous cross fire or were overtaken by fleet footed runners. Others threw away their arms and ran frantically along the road. They were headed off by mount-ed Indians and sought concealment in the woods. When overtaken, most of these were ruthlessly shot down. The homeless Pottowatomies slaked their thirst for revenge and spared few. Fifteen men of the 17th United States Infantry, under Lieut. Garrett, threw down their arms in a body, but were all killed, except the officer. Of that regiment. one hundred and twenty were killed and only sixty taken prisoners.

The Christianised Wyandots were more merciful. Winchester with his son, a lad of sixteen, and Colonel Lewis, after a pursuit of nearly three miles, surrendered to Roundhead, who stripped the general of his richly laced uniform coat and put it on himself. Among the of-ficers slain were Colonel Allen and Captain Simpson, a member of Congress. A wounded officer and a few men ran down towards the lake and succeeded in concealing themselves until night fell, when they made their way back to the encampment at the Miami. Oth-ers shut themselves up in detached houses or barns, where they were surrounded and eventually killed or made prisoners. In storming one

77. Narrative of Shadrach Byfield, 41st Regiment.

of these buildings, Lieut.-Colonel St. George received four severe wounds which rendered him incapable of further active service during the war.

Meanwhile, the guns in the orchard were gradually advanced across the hollow until they were within fifty yards of the palisades, without effecting a breach or making much impression. The shells from the howitzers had failed to set tire to the snow-covered houses against which they were directed. The gunners and their escort, clearly silhouetted against the snowy surface of the ground, fell fast under the opposing rifle fire. The only sergeant and one private of the Royal Artillery were killed: Lieut. Troughton and seven rank and file were wounded, Bombardier Kitson, who had behaved so well in the last action, dying of his wounds soon after. One seaman was killed and three officers and thirteen seamen were wounded. Lieut. Rolette received a charge of buckshot in the side, and a musket ball spent its force in the folds of a handkerchief he had wound about his head to relieve the pain of a severe headache.[78] Midshipman Richardson, a boy of fourteen, lost a leg. The horse and driver of a sled brining forward ammunition were both shot.

The guns were silenced and the most advanced piece of abandoned within twenty-five or thirty yards of the palisades. Some American riflemen leaped over the fence to take possession, but were driven back by the fire of the escort. Lieut. Robert Irvine then ran forward alone and, seizing the drag-rope, hauled it to a place of safety, amid a shower of bullets, receiving a severe wound in the foot. Procter witnessed this gallant act and subsequently testified his admiration in a letter of thanks, assuring him that he should lose no opportunity of suitably rewarding him.[79] The men who were still unhurt were so benumbed by the cold that they could scarcely work the guns. The escort had lost one-third of its number. Ensign Thomas Kerr, a gallant boy of eighteen, had fallen mortally wounded in leading an assault on a large barn occupied by the enemy's riflemen, encouraging his men with his last words to push on.

Captain Tallon then formed the 41st into column of sections and made a most determined effort to force his way into the village. Every rifle that could be brought to bear, not only from the loopholes, but the windows of the houses on either flank, was directed upon them with such effect that within half an hour fifteen privates were killed

---

78. P. Bender, *Old and New Canada*.
79. Troughton to Irvine, 28 January, 1813.

and Captain Tallon, Lieut. Clemow, three sergeants and ninety-two rank and file were wounded, being nearly one-half of the entire detachment. The attack was then discontinued until the militia and Indians could be reassembled. Exasperated by the sight of the slaughter of their comrades outside, some of the American riflemen continued to fire upon the wounded whenever they attempted to get away, and were even seen to use their knives and tomahawks upon them. This naturally excited the bitter resentment of the troops watching them from the shelter of the hollow, who became eager to retaliate.[80]

As the firing had nearly ceased, the defenders of the village sallied out and set fire to a barn which had been occupied by a party of Indians. Bread was distributed among them and ammunition served out.

The Indians gradually returned, some of them with bleeding scalps dangling from their saddles, others driving prisoners before them.[81] Among these were General Winchester, Colonel Lewis and other officers, who were conducted to Colonel Procter.

The investment of the village was completed, and a party of Indians getting into the bed of the river and sheltering themselves beneath the bank, began a fire from the rear, which struck down several men. Preparations were in progress to set some of the houses on fire and thus drive out the defenders. Winchester was not unnaturally dispirited and appalled by the slaughter of so many of his men which he had already witnessed, and saw little hope for the remainder, who were completely surrounded. If their position was carried by assault, few could expect to escape death, as the Indians, and indeed the British regular troops and militia, were greatly exasperated. He asked Procter if they would be given an opportunity to surrender, and received the reply that they must decide quickly, as he intended to set the place on fire at once and could then take no responsibility for the conduct of the Indians. But he assured him that if they surrendered at discretion, without further delay, he would make every effort to protect them and the officers would be permitted to retain their swords and private property.

Winchester then directed Captain Overton, his *aide-de-camp*, to go with a flag of truce to the commanding officer of the troops in the village and deliver an order to surrender. Procter himself, with some other officers, accompanied Overton to make sure that no time was

---

80. Procter to Sheaffe, 1st February. 1813; John Richardson to Charles Askin. 4th February, 1813; Byfield, *Narrative*.
81. Atherton, 47.

lost and there could be no misunderstanding. Major George Madison, afterwards Governor of Kentucky, who was the senior officer, came forward to meet them attended by Brigade Major Garrard. They expressed surprise to learn that General Winchester was a prisoner and seemed reluctant to obey the order to surrender without conditions. Procter insisted that they must consent to this, as all he could promise was protection for their lives and property as far as his power extended. He seems to have given them clearly to understand that the Indians were greatly infuriated and that he was doubtful whether he could restrain them in any event.

Madison returned to the village to consult his officers. He found that he had lost about forty in killed and wounded, reducing his effective force to 384 of all ranks. Major Graves, his second in command, Captain Hart and several other officers were among the wounded. The men had but two or three cartridges apiece. They were surrounded by much superior numbers. The buildings they occupied were inflammable. A retreat was impossible, and there was no hope of a reinforcement in time to save them. A decision to surrender was soon arrived at. When this was announced to the men there were the usual disorderly scenes. Cries of rage were uttered and rifles dashed furiously to the ground.[82]

When Madison signified his intention of obeying Winchester's order Procter was unquestionably relieved of much anxiety. More than two-fifths of his regular force had already been killed or wounded. A continuation of the contest meant further bloodshed, resulting most probably in the complete extermination of the enemy's force. Some of the Indians had already shown an inclination to kill the wounded and strip the prisoners in the most unequivocal manner. He readily assured Madison that he would endeavour to protect his sick and wounded and prevent pillage; but remarked that his own wounded were numerous and must be removed from the field first. He accordingly advised him to place such of his men as were unable to march to Amherstburg in charge of his surgeons, and a guard would be detailed to remain with them.

The prisoners had scarcely been disarmed when an Indian scout reported that he had discovered the advance guard of an American reinforcement on the road to the Miami only eight or ten miles distant. No time must be lost in sending them away and removing the

<hr>

82. Procter to Sheaffe, 25th January, 1813; Winchester to Secretary of War, January 26 and February 11, 1813; Atherton, 50-2; McAfee, 213, 216.

wounded. He had but a single surgeon and very few sleighs. Every man that was able to walk was accordingly ordered to make the best of his way to the bivouac of the night before at Swan Creek, where a rest camp would be formed.[83]

So little apprehension was felt at this time for the safety of the wounded prisoners that several of them who were slightly hurt and perfectly able to march decided to remain behind, possibly in the hope of regaining their liberty. The entire number of prisoners thus left at Frenchtown was about sixty-four, including five surgeons. Among them were Major Graves. Major Woolfolk, Winchester's secretary, and Captains Hart and Hickman. Captain Matthew Elliott, of the Indian Department, had been a classmate of Hart at Princeton College, and promised to send a sleigh next day to convey him with other wounded officers to Amherstburg. Major Reynolds, with three interpreters, remained with them as a safeguard against straggling Indians. Lieut.-Colonel St. George and others whose wounds were severe and the whole of the British dead were left behind for several hours until sleighs could be secured for their removal.[84]

Procter had lost in all twenty-four killed and 158 wounded, being more than two-fifths of his entire white force. Among the wounded were twelve officers. The number of prisoners greatly exceeded that of his effective troops. Captain William Caldwell and Interpreter John Wilson, of the Indian Department, were also wounded: but the loss of the Indians seems to have been inconsiderable, probably not exceeding four or five warriors killed. Not more than four hundred stands of arms and a small quantity of stores were secured, the remainder having been instantly carried off by the Indians. The first official return of prisoners dated January 25th, showed a total of thirty-three officers, twenty-seven sergeants and 435 rank and file. Winchester's official letter increased the number to thirty-five officers and 487 non-commissioned officers and men, which his return of February 11th still further augmented to thirty-seven officers and 500 N.C.O. and privates. Twenty-two officers and 375 N.C.O. and privates were returned as killed or missing. (See list following)

Staff.—Wounded, Lieut.-Colonel St. George, severely.

Royal Artillery.—Killed, one sergeant, one gunner; wounded, Lieut. Troughton, one corporal, five gunners, one bombardier.

83. Byfield, Narrative: Atherton, 67.
84. Coffin, 205-6.

10th Royal Veteran Battalion.—Wounded, two privates.

41st Regiment.—Killed, fifteen privates; wounded, Captain Tallon, Lieut. Clemow, three sergeants, one corporal, 91 privates.

Royal Newfoundland Regiment—Killed, one private; wounded, Ensign Kerr, three sergeants, three corporals, thirteen privates.

Marine Department—Killed, one seaman; wounded, Lieuts. Rolette and Irvine, Midshipman Richardson, one gunner, twelve seamen.

1st Essex Militia.—Killed, two privates; wounded, Captain Mills, Lieuts. McCormick and Gordon, two sergeants and seven privates.

2nd Essex Militia.—Killed, three privates; wounded. Ensign Gouin and three privates.

Killed and missing:—

17th United States Infantry—One surgeon, two captains, three lieutenants, two ensigns, 112 N.C.O. and privates.

1st Regiment Kentucky Militia.—One major, one captain, one surgeons mate, one ensign, 36 N C O. and privates.

1st Kentucky Rifles.—One lieutenant-colonel, one surgeon, four captains, one ensign, 154 N.C.O. and privates.

5th Regimen Kentucky Militia.—One major, one captain, one lieutenant, 73 N.C.O. and privates.

Prisoners:—

17th United States Infantry.—One captain, two lieutenants, three ensigns, 54 N.C.O. and privates.

1st Kentucky Militia.—Two captains, one lieutenant, one ensign, 104 N.C.O. and privates, of whom one ensign and five privates were wounded.

1st Kentucky Rifles.—One major, two captains, four ensigns, 133 N.C.O. and privates, of whom two ensigns and six privates were wounded.

5th Kentucky Militia.—One lieut.-colonel, one adjutant, one quartermaster, one surgeon, one surgeon's mate, three captains, one lieutenant, four ensigns, 180 N.C.O. and privates, of whom one sergeant, three corporals and seven privates were wounded.

2nd Kentucky Militia.—One captain, twenty privates.

Brigade Staff.—One brigadier-general, one brigade inspector, one *aide-de-camp*, one lieutenant 17th United States Infantry.

Of these reported killed or missing, twenty-five or thirty, including three officers, made their escape to the Miami. Forty or fifty others were carried off as prisoners by the Indians, most of whom were delivered up or ransomed in the course of six months, through the efforts of the officers of that department. Quite three hundred were killed, and the small number of wounded prisoners sufficiently indicate the merciless character of the pursuit.

The worst was yet to come. During the night a number of Indians intent on plunder stealthily returned to the River Raisin. Major Reynolds and two of the interpreters had been called away and but one remained, who was unfortunately not proficient in their language. The Indians ransacked the village and found a quantity of liquor Many of them became drunk and began to rob and insult the wounded. The interpreter and surgeons were helpless. Words were succeeded by blows, and finally these wretches killed Captains Hart and Hickman and several privates who were unable to walk and carried off the remainder with the surgeons as prisoners. Several others whose strength failed on the march were instantly butchered. Not more than half the wounded left here eventually escaped death in this manner.[85]

It is, perhaps, not surprising that Procter was personally blamed for this massacre by his enemies, and indeed, he seems to have anticipated censure,

> My opinion of the enemy is not more favourable than it was from what I have seen and heard of them. They were armed with knives and tomahawks, and some of them used them. They fired at the wounded as they lay on the ground, themselves behind enclosures and in buildings. Every art, every means have been employed to prejudice and influence these misguided people against us. There have been some instances, I am sorry to say, of Indian barbarity; but the example was set by the enemy they came to seek. I know we shall be vilified, for the truth is not in them. I have not anything to accuse myself of.[86]

---

85. Am. State Papers, Military Affairs, I, 367-75; Atherton, 70-5.
86. Procter to Sheaffe, 1st February, 1813.

In evidence of this he enclosed an extract of letter written to him from Sandwich on January 29 by General Winchester, in which that officer said:

> You will please to be assured, sir, that I feel a high sense of gratitude for the polite attention shown to myself as well as for the humanity and kindness with which you have caused the prisoners to be treated who fell into your hands on the 22nd instant. [87]

The appearance of these men generally was uncouth and repellent. They were haggard and unshaven. Their clothing was tattered and dirty with many months' wear. Numbers of them still wore the grimy linen hunting frocks and trousers they had on when they marched from Kentucky in midsummer. Blankets were wrapped about their waists to protect them from the cold and kept in place by broad leather belts, in which were suspended large knives and tomahawks. Their long, tangled locks were covered with shabby slouched hats. Some wore leather stocks with a metal badge representing an eagle picking out the eyes of a lion. The great majority seemed sullen and dejected; but some maintained an appearance of bravado and defiance, one of whom excited peals of laughter from his captors by exclaiming in a tone of amazement, "Well! You have taken the greatest set of game-cocks that ever came from Kentuck!"[88]

There were no buildings at Amherstburg adequate for the accommodation of so many prisoners, and on the night of the 23rd all but the officers were penned in a woodyard exposed to a chilling rain, if they were paroled and sent home by the route they had advanced, the poverty of his means of defence would at once be disclosed, and probably other troops upon the line of communication would be liberated to renew the attack. The Indians proposed that some of them should be offered in exchange for the Wyandots detained at Sandusky, but Procter deemed this scarcely expedient.

Yet it was necessary to get rid of them immediately, as he could neither house them, feed them, nor furnish the necessary guards without great difficulty. He accordingly determined to march them overland to Niagara, to be there paroled or forwarded to Quebec. On January 25th they were marched to Sandwich, where the wounded and others declared unfit for the journey were detained and lodged in

---

87. Winchester to Procter, 29th January, 1813.
88. Atherton, 54: Richardson, 140; Darnell, 72.

the court-house in charge of the sheriff.[89]

Procter's first act on his return was to write to General Sheaffe in the most urgent terms to send him a reinforcement of at least one company of regulars to make good his loss in the action. This was done with such promptitude that the light company of the 41st met the prisoners at Oxford and arrived at Amherstburg on February 7.

Meanwhile he had learned with much alarm that a number of the inhabitants of "that depot of treachery, Detroit," had formed a plot to overpower the militia garrison and make themselves masters of the fort while he was engaged at the River Raisin. The rapidity of his movements had alone prevented the execution of this design and it became known to him soon after his return. A letter from Woodward to Monroe was intercepted, which decided Procter to remove him from office as "an artful, designing, ambitious young man" who was endeavouring to "ingratiate himself with his own government and to court popularity."

The Territory of Michigan was placed under martial law and one hundred and four of "the more suspicious and turbulent characters", among them Captain Brevoort and William Macomb, whose son was a colonel in the United States army, were ordered to proceed under military escort to Niagara. A few of these were British subjects; but the majority had actually become prisoners of war under the capitulation and had given their parole.[90] A report that Harrison had again advanced to the Miami with an overwhelming force emboldened twenty-nine of these malcontents to meet and pass a series of resolutions protesting against this order as "an unjustifiable and wanton invasion of private rights," and "a flagrant and gross violation of the third article of the capitulation." They declared their intention of maintaining a "strict and exemplary neutrality," adding that if there were any among them " whose conduct and behaviour does not strictly comport with the spirit and meaning of the preceding resolution they ought not to be screened from punishment."

Woodward was requested to present these resolutions to Colonel Procter and urge him to revoke the obnoxious order. He took advantage of this opportunity to complain that some of the prisoners and some inhabitants had been killed by the Indians since the action at Frenchtown, and some houses burnt, and to propose a new convention on behalf of the residents of Detroit. He asked that a mili-

89. Wm. Hands to ———.
90. Procter to Sheaffe, 4th February, 1813; Farmer, *History of Detroit.*

tary force should be stationed there to protect the inhabitants "from slaughter, conflagration and plunder" and that they should be armed and organized for their own defence. All Indians should be prohibited from entering the region extending from the River Aux Ecorces to Grosse Point and from carrying scalps through the town. Procter was requested to name eighteen persons from whom they would choose six as hostages, while they would name eighteen from whom he might select six to act as commissioners "to apprehend all persons who should violate their neutrality or give rise to probable suspicion thereof." This agreement should then be submitted to the American commander for his ratification. Woodward cited the conventions adopted by Montgomery at Montreal and the Marquis de Bouillé at Tobago in support of his proposal.

Procter was greatly enraged. He declared that Woodward's letter was "insolent" and that the resolutions were "indecent," and ordered the deportation of the suspects to be put into effect without delay. Woodward was required to name a day to substantiate his charges respecting the murder of prisoners. Many residents of Detroit were British subjects by birth, and Procter now proposed to arm for their own defence all who were willing to take the oath of allegiance, while an oath of neutrality would be required from "confirmed citizens of the United States."

His situation was still extremely precarious, as Harrison had actually advanced to the Miami and might at any time he expected to move upon Amherstburg with more thousands of troops than he had hundreds to oppose them. The Indians and militia might indeed he relied on for support as long as there was some probability of success; but a reverse would dishearten and disperse them. He had already witnes.sed the powerful effects of hope and fear on the minds of both. His influence over the Indians in particular, largely depended upon their estimate of his strength, and he declared that not le.ss than an entire regiment of regular troops would he necessary to ensure the safety of the military posts and shipping.[91]

He had shown conspicuous energy and decision on all occasions and there seemed little reason to suspect that he would be found wanting in future.

Woodward, who had excellent opportunities of observation and

91. Conditions proposed for convention; Woodward to Procter, 2nd February, 1813; Procter to Sheaffc, 4th February, 1813; Procter to Baynes, 31st January, 1813: Procter to Sheaffe. 2nd February, 1813.

was a keen and by no means a friendly critic, wrote with unrestrained admiration:

> The operations of the British commander are marked with the same minute correctness of judgment in this instance and the same boldness of conception and execution which distinguished in the former instance his illustrious predecessor, General Brock. It is a military movement of equal and in fact of greater splendour.[92]

---

92. Woodward to Monroe, 31st January, 1813.

LEONAUR

ALSO FROM LEONAUR
AVAILABLE IN SOFTCOVER OR HARDCOVER WITH DUST JACKET

LIFE IN THE ARMY OF NORTHERN VIRGINIA by *Carlton McCarthy*—The Observations of a Confederate Artilleryman of Cutshaw's Battalion During the American Civil War 1861-1865.

HISTORY OF THE CAVALRY OF THE ARMY OF THE POTOMAC by *Charles D. Rhodes*—Including Pope's Army of Virginia and the Cavalry Operations in West Virginia During the American Civil War.

CAMP-FIRE AND COTTON-FIELD by *Thomas W. Knox*—A New York Herald Correspondent's View of the American Civil War.

SERGEANT STILLWELL by *Leander Stillwell* —The Experiences of a Union Army Soldier of the 61st Illinois Infantry During the American Civil War.

STONEWALL'S CANNONEER by *Edward A. Moore*—Experiences with the Rockbridge Artillery, Confederate Army of Northern Virginia, During the American Civil War.

THE SIXTH CORPS by *George Stevens*—The Army of the Potomac, Union Army, During the American Civil War.

THE RAILROAD RAIDERS by *William Pittenger*—An Ohio Volunteers Recollections of the Andrews Raid to Disrupt the Confederate Railroad in Georgia During the American Civil War.

CITIZEN SOLDIER by *John Beatty*—An Account of the American Civil War by a Union Infantry Officer of Ohio Volunteers Who Became a Brigadier General.

COX: PERSONAL RECOLLECTIONS OF THE CIVIL WAR--VOLUME 1 by *Jacob Dolson Cox*—West Virginia, Kanawha Valley, Gauley Bridge, Cotton Mountain, South Mountain, Antietam, the Morgan Raid & the East Tennessee Campaign.

COX: PERSONAL RECOLLECTIONS OF THE CIVIL WAR--VOLUME 2 by *Jacob Dolson Cox*—Siege of Knoxville, East Tennessee, Atlanta Campaign, the Nashville Campaign & the North Carolina Campaign.

KERSHAW'S BRIGADE VOLUME 1 by *D. Augustus Dickert*—Manassas, Seven Pines, Sharpsburg (Antietam), Fredricksburg, Chancellorsville, Gettysburg, Chickamauga, Chattanooga, Fort Sanders & Bean Station.

KERSHAW'S BRIGADE VOLUME 2 by *D. Augustus Dickert*—At the wilderness, Cold Harbour, Petersburg, The Shenandoah Valley and Cedar Creek..

LEONAUR

ALSO FROM LEONAUR
AVAILABLE IN SOFTCOVER OR HARDCOVER WITH DUST JACKET

THE RELUCTANT REBEL by *William G. Stevenson*—A young Kentuckian's experiences in the Confederate Infantry & Cavalry during the American Civil War..

BOOTS AND SADDLES by *Elizabeth B. Custer*—The experiences of General Custer's Wife on the Western Plains.

FANNIE BEERS' CIVIL WAR by *Fannie A. Beers*—A Confederate Lady's Experiences of Nursing During the Campaigns & Battles of the American Civil War.

LADY SALE'S AFGHANISTAN by *Florentia Sale*—An Indomitable Victorian Lady's Account of the Retreat from Kabul During the First Afghan War.

THE TWO WARS OF MRS DUBERLY by *Frances Isabella Duberly*—An Intrepid Victorian Lady's Experience of the Crimea and Indian Mutiny.

THE REBELLIOUS DUCHESS by *Paul F. S. Dermoncourt*—The Adventures of the Duchess of Berri and Her Attempt to Overthrow French Monarchy.

LADIES OF WATERLOO by *Charlotte A. Eaton, Magdalene de Lancey & Juana Smith*—The Experiences of Three Women During the Campaign of 1815: Waterloo Days by Charlotte A. Eaton, A Week at Waterloo by Magdalene de Lancey & Juana's Story by Juana Smith.

TWO YEARS BEFORE THE MAST by *Richard Henry Dana. Jr.*—The account of one young man's experiences serving on board a sailing brig—the Penelope—bound for California, between the years 1834-36.

A SAILOR OF KING GEORGE by *Frederick Hoffman*—From Midshipman to Captain—Recollections of War at Sea in the Napoleonic Age 1793-1815.

LORDS OF THE SEA by *A. T. Mahan*—Great Captains of the Royal Navy During the Age of Sail.

COGGESHALL'S VOYAGES: VOLUME 1 by *George Coggeshall*—The Recollections of an American Schooner Captain.

COGGESHALL'S VOYAGES: VOLUME 2 by *George Coggeshall*—The Recollections of an American Schooner Captain.

TWILIGHT OF EMPIRE by *Sir Thomas Ussher & Sir George Cockburn*—Two accounts of Napoleon's Journeys in Exile to Elba and St. Helena: Narrative of Events by Sir Thomas Ussher & Napoleon's Last Voyage: Extract of a diary by Sir George Cockburn.

LEONAUR

ALSO FROM LEONAUR
AVAILABLE IN SOFTCOVER OR HARDCOVER WITH DUST JACKET

THE 9TH—THE KING'S (LIVERPOOL REGIMENT) IN THE GREAT WAR 1914 - 1918 *by Enos H. G. Roberts*—Mersey to mud—war and Liverpool men.

THE GAMBARDIER *by Mark Severn*—The experiences of a battery of Heavy artillery on the Western Front during the First World War.

FROM MESSINES TO THIRD YPRES *by Thomas Floyd*—A personal account of the First World War on the Western front by a 2/5th Lancashire Fusilier.

THE IRISH GUARDS IN THE GREAT WAR - VOLUME 1 *by Rudyard Kipling*—Edited and Compiled from Their Diaries and Papers—The First Battalion.

THE IRISH GUARDS IN THE GREAT WAR - VOLUME 1 *by Rudyard Kipling*—Edited and Compiled from Their Diaries and Papers—The Second Battalion.

ARMOURED CARS IN EDEN *by K. Roosevelt*—An American President's son serving in Rolls Royce armoured cars with the British in Mesopatamia & with the American Artillery in France during the First World War.

CHASSEUR OF 1914 *by Marcel Dupont*—Experiences of the twilight of the French Light Cavalry by a young officer during the early battles of the great war in Europe.

TROOP HORSE & TRENCH *by R.A. Lloyd*—The experiences of a British Lifeguardsman of the household cavalry fighting on the western front during the First World War 1914-18.

THE EAST AFRICAN MOUNTED RIFLES *by C.J. Wilson*—Experiences of the campaign in the East African bush during the First World War.

THE LONG PATROL *by George Berrie*—A Novel of Light Horsemen from Gallipoli to the Palestine campaign of the First World War.

THE FIGHTING CAMELIERS *by Frank Reid*—The exploits of the Imperial Camel Corps in the desert and Palestine campaigns of the First World War.

STEEL CHARIOTS IN THE DESERT *by S. C. Rolls*—The first world war experiences of a Rolls Royce armoured car driver with the Duke of Westminster in Libya and in Arabia with T.E. Lawrence.

WITH THE IMPERIAL CAMEL CORPS IN THE GREAT WAR *by Geoffrey Inchbald*—The story of a serving officer with the British 2nd battalion against the Senussi and during the Palestine campaign.

Lightning Source UK Ltd.
Milton Keynes UK
UKOW02f2002210317

297155UK00001B/96/P

9 781782 821335